MAP
OF THE
SOUL:
7

Persona, Shadow & Ego in the World of BTS

MURRAY STEIN
with
Steven Buser & Leonard Cruz

CHIRON PUBLICATIONS • ASHEVILLE, N.C.

www.ChironPublications.com

Interior design by Danijela Mijailovic
Cover design by Tijana Mijailovic

Printed primarily in the United States of America.
ISBN 978-1-63051-850-9 paperback
ISBN 978-1-63051-851-6 hardcover
ISBN 978-1-63051-852-3 electronic
ISBN 978-1-63051-853-0 limited edition paperback

Library of Congress Cataloging-in-Publication Data

Names: Stein, Murray, 1943- author. | Buser, Steven, 1963- author. | Cruz, Leonard, 1957- author.
Title: Map of the soul - 7 : persona, shadow & ego in the world of BTS / Murray Stein; with Steven Buser & Leonard Cruz.
Description: Asheville, N.C. : Chiron Publications, [2020] | Series: Map of the soul series ; volume 4 | Includes bibliographical references. | Summary: "Beyond summarizing the three volumes on Persona, Shadow and Ego in the Map of the Soul series, this latest book explores the entire BTS album, start to finish, revealing profound insights into the collective psyche of BTS. The title of BTS's latest album, Map of the Soul: 7, captivates the mind with its suggestive and alluring imagery. It came as a surprise to many fans. Expected was an album that would follow upon Map of the Soul: Persona with songs about Shadow or Ego. While the new album does indeed include songs with these themes, it is much more complex and broader in vision than expected. The number 7 suggests mystery. It catches the mind's attention with its symbolic significance. What does this number mean in relation to the idea of a "map of the soul?" This book dives into this mystery and explores the unconscious reaches of our mind. Fans of BTS from around the world will marvel at the depth of meaning in the songs contained in Map of the Soul: 7. They take the listener into deep reflection upon the meaning of striving and ambition, the dangers of worldly success, and the amazing resiliency of the human spirit to recover and go on despite the pitfalls on life's journey. The songs themselves function as a map for souls who are setting out in life and engaging in challenging relationships. The songs are reflective, mirroring what we find within ourselves in our struggles to become and to thrive. When you stand on the threshold of a new land, it is useful to have a map as your guide. The great psychologist of the 20th Century, Carl Jung, created a Map of the Soul that many people in his time found more than a little helpful, even lifesaving. It is even more so now, for people in the 21st Century, caught in the profound complexities of modern life. Armed with this map, people are better able to find their way successfully through life's journey. Today, BTS is putting this map into the hands of their fans. For this great service we are profoundly very grateful"-- Provided by publisher.
Identifiers: LCCN 2020021941 (print) | LCCN 2020021942 (ebook) | ISBN 9781630518509 (v. 4 ; paperback) | ISBN 9781630518516 (v. 4 ; hardcover) | ISBN 9781630518530 (v. 4 ; limited edition paperback) | ISBN 9781630518523 (v. 4 ; electronic)
Subjects: LCSH: Persona (Psychoanalysis) | Shadow (Psychoanalysis) | Ego (Psychology) | BTS (Musical group)
Classification: LCC BF175.5.P47 S745 2020 (print) | LCC BF175.5.P47 (ebook) | DDC 155.2--dc23
LC record available at https://lccn.loc.gov/2020021941
LC ebook record available at https://lccn.loc.gov/2020021942

To BTS and their
ARMY of fans

Special thanks to *BTS ARMY*,
Carla Postma-Slabbekoorn at the
ARMY Help Center, Laura London
at *Speaking of Jung*, Tijana Mijailovic
and to BTS for bringing Jungian
psychology to a new generation.

Table of Contents

Preface

The title of BTS's latest album, *Map of the Soul: 7*, sticks to the mind because it is suggestive and enigmatic. It came as a surprise to many fans. Expected was an album that would follow upon *Map of the Soul: Persona* with songs about Shadow or Ego. The new album does indeed include songs with these themes, but it is more complex and broader in vision than expected. The number 7 suggests a mystery. And this catches the mind's attention and stays there because this number is symbolically significant. One wants to know more. What does this number mean in relation to the idea of a "map of the soul"? In the pages that follow I attempt to understand something about this mystery, and I hope the reader will be incited to continue thinking about it as well.

This album was released at an exceptional and historic moment in our century, namely at the beginning of the outbreak of the coronavirus pandemic. Is this a meaningful coincidence, as we say a "synchronicity"? One of the songs in the album, "Black Swan," especially caught my eye. When I first saw this number performed online, the world was just beginning to become aware of the coronavirus threat and its potentially devastating effect on the entire global community. Like a "black swan event," it was not only an unexpected guest but an unwanted one. In my view, this song signaled the emergence of the Shadow over all of humanity, threatening life itself and filling many people with a paralyzing fear of catastrophe. At the moment I saw the film clip, I thought to myself: Is this album going to turn out to be a mirror image of an archetypal event in human history? The black swan is an anomaly, and in common parlance the phrase refers to an unpredicted dire event that sweeps over us out of nowhere and covers us with its shadow of destruction. We were about to enter the valley of the shadow of death, so brilliantly depicted in the film and the song. As it turned out, the song was an early harbinger of what was to come.

Fans of BTS around the world will marvel at the depth of meaning in the songs contained in *Map of the Soul : 7*. They can take the listener to a level of deep reflection upon the meaning of striving and ambition, the dangers and emptiness of worldly success, and the amazing resiliency of the human spirit to recover and go on despite the many pitfalls that beset us on our life's journey. The songs themselves function as a map for souls who are setting out in life and encounter themselves in the complexity of their relationships with others. The songs are reflective, mirroring what we find within ourselves in our struggles to become and to thrive.

As a Jungian psychoanalyst of another generation, I applaud the teaching BTS is offering to the new generation entering into the presently bewildering world of adulthood. When you stand on the threshold of a new land, it is useful to have a map as your guide. The great psychologist of the 20th century, Carl Jung, created a map of the soul that many people in his time found more than a little helpful, even lifesaving. It is even more so, I believe, for people in the 21st century because of its depth of understanding this territory that we call the human psyche. Armed with his map, people are better able to find their way successfully through life's journey. Today, BTS is putting this map into the hands of its fans. For this great service, I am personally very grateful.

Murray Stein
Goldiwil, Switzerland
April 11, 2020

Chapter 1

BTS and the Number 7

By Murray Stein

It was somewhat of a surprise when BTS titled the current album *Map of the Soul: 7*. Many of us were expecting them to continue along the lines of their last release, *Map of the Soul: Persona*, and proceed with either *Map of the Soul: Shadow* or *Map of the Soul: Ego*. *Map of the Soul: 7* was both creative and unexpected.

BTS choosing the number 7 can be looked at in a number of ways. The obvious reasons are that there are 7 members of the band and that they've been together for 7 years. But the number 7 is symbolic in a larger sense as well. For instance, we have 7 days in the week. That's not arbitrary. It derives from the biblical text, where God is shown to have created the world in 6 days and to have rested on the 7th. The number 7 completes things. It is a number that brings us to a sense that a creative act is finished, something immensely significant has been done, and now it is time to take a rest. One can think about it in a number of different ways, but I think in reference to this album, it seems to indicate BTS is finished with something. They are finished with a hugely creative phase. They have accomplished their work, and now they are going to take a look in retrospect and admire what has been achieved.

7 as a Prime Number

Another angle of reflection suggests itself. 7 is a prime number, and prime numbers are divisible only by one and themselves. The album's title signifies that BTS is a single entity, unbreakable. They are a prime number, and they've worked hard to bring their group to such a point. They live together, they spend practically all their waking hours together, they identify strongly with the same ideas, music, style of living, etc. In a sense, BTS is a single personality made up of seven (fast) moving parts. Of course, you wonder how long this can go on before they will feel the need to live their own separate and individual lives. In that case, 7 would become

1+1+1+1+1+1+1. The day will come when this singular unit of 7 will break apart and perhaps subsequently reformulate the individuals as another kind of unit, perhaps more complex, with more individual features allowed to the personalities in the group. But they've worked very hard to form a prime singularity as a group, and now they are celebrating it even as they are subtly anticipating a different future.

The Seven Numbers in the Individuation Process

In Jungian Psychology, the number 7 is often associated with the alchemist Maria Prophetissa. Maria Prophetissa is a legendary early alchemist of the first centuries of the Common Era. She describes a formula, sometimes referred to as the *Axiom of Maria Prophetissa* stating: "One becomes two, two becomes three, and out of the three comes the one as the fourth." When you add the three to the four, of course, you get 7.

Each of the numbers from One to Seven has a symbolic psychological meaning. "One" is the first and original state of consciousness, the beginning. It is what Jung called the *Pleroma*. "All is One"—there is no differentiation in this state of the personality. It is the original state of wholeness that we come into the world with at birth. This contains the entire potential for the personality that has yet to be developed in time and space.

"Two" results when there is the first differentiation in consciousness. Where there was One before, now there are Two. This signifies consciousness of a distinction between self and other. This is an advance of the person, seen developmentally: The child discovers the difference between itself and others. Consciousness is beginning to do its work, which is the making of distinctions, and this continues as the sense of a person's individual identity grows stronger. The number Two also indicates the division between consciousness and the unconscious. Consciousness is emerging from the waters of the unconscious and creating a perception of the differentiated world of objects, outer and inner.

Out of these two elements in the psyche, which are sometimes in conflict with one another, a third function emerges: cognitive thinking and imagination. The conflict arises between the instinctual pressures for fulfillment of needs and desires on the one hand and the "reality principle" (the ego) on the other. The third function finds a way to bridge over the two and create new possibilities. "Three" represents the possibility for abstract thinking and planning. This is the birth of the Spirit and is responsible for culture. Language becomes a tool for thinking and communicating, and with this come abstract possibilities like the naming of groups and imagining things that do not exist. Three means consciousness of possibilities that hover above the Earth; it is rich with ideals, abstract values, and possibilities for future development.

Now the fourth element is needed. When Four appears in the formula, it means that the ideas, ideals and possibilities created in the Three can become grounded in reality and be actualized. The number Four is often associated with the Feminine and with the Earth. The movement from Three to Four represents a movement toward the grounding of thought and imagined projects in time and space: The city gets founded, the academic degree is achieved, the business is set up and begins functioning.

The number Five represents the *"quinta essentia,"* the essential core of the personality. The achievement of the Five means that achievements and developments have been realized and now it is possible to discover this essential core of the Self and to relate to it consciously. In a way, this is a return to the One, only now the whole is more conscious.

The number Six represents the union of opposites, masculine and feminine. Consciousness and the unconscious are united. Jung called this the *mysterium coniunctionis*, and his last extensive book bears this title. This is a stage of consolidation of what has been achieved in the earlier stages of development. It is a huge achievement and a rare one.

After that we arrive at the number Seven, a holy number, a number of transcendence and ultimate completion of a journey begun with the number One. In the Bible, the seventh day is the day of rest, and it arrives after the previous six days of development, differentiation, and creation of consciousness. This is shown in the image of a *triangle placed in a square*, the Three within the Four. This Seven represents the sense of spiritual completion. This is the individuated personality.

The movement from One to Seven represents the full individuation process.

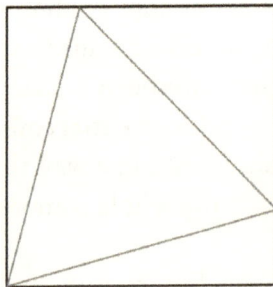

Chapter 2

Reflections on the Lyrics of BTS' Map of the Soul: 7

By Murray Stein

It is well known that BTS's concept of Map of the Soul is based on Dr. Murray Stein's writings. This chapter analyzes the lyrics in *Map of the Soul: 7* from Dr. Stein's approach as a Jungian psychoanalyst. It was adapted from interviews with Murray Stein conducted by Laura London on the podcast *Speaking of Jung: Interviews with Jungian Analysts*; Episodes 44, 53, 54 & 55.

Map of the Soul: 7, Suffering, and BTS

Map of the Soul: 7 breaks into new territory for BTS. They are breaking out of the stereotypical persona of a successful K-pop boy's band and revealing their deeper nature to us. Although many of their fans might not see it, BTS has suffered and struggled. They've worked extraordinarily hard to get to where they are, and they've suffered along the way. They've had their ups and downs, yet people likely don't see that. All they see is the bright lights of the entertainment on-stage—the beautiful smiles, the colorful hair, the clothes, the acrobatic dancing. But in this album, BTS is saying, "We're human beings behind this entertainment facade. It's a mask. We're real people, we have a history, and we have struggles, we've suffered." This message comes through in this album, loud and clear.

Beyond the suffering, however, there's also a theme of resilience, of overcoming their problems and setbacks. Ultimately, it's a very affirming album. It reveals the suffering and the reality behind the persona, but it also affirms the resilience of the group. The song *We Are Bulletproof: The Eternal* is sung to their ARMY. They have been tremendously supported by their fans. They've survived and come through, and they're singing about it. The album is celebratory as well as revealing of their pain and struggles.

BTS, Rebirth and Transformation

All of us go through phases of transition and transformation in our lives. Carl Jung described this as the individuation process. There are several critical developmental periods. The transformation during adolescence from childhood to adulthood is the most obvious. Again at midlife, there is a transformation from early adulthood to mature adulthood, and then late in life there is another transformation into old age. These are death and rebirth experiences. The old identity dies and a new one is born.

We have to shed our old identities at certain key moments in life, the way a snake sheds its skin. As the snake grows, the skin becomes too small for it and needs to be shed. We also outgrow our forms sometimes, like when our baby teeth fall out. People often dream of losing their teeth, and that's a part of the growth process. They're losing their old concepts, their old way of digesting their experiences, and they're going to have to wait awhile until new teeth grow in place. Just as we experience this on a physical level, it occurs on the psychological level as well. The psyche goes through its processes of shedding the old skin when the old identity doesn't fit anymore. People experience this in relationships. For a while a relationship feels "just perfect," but then it becomes tedious and doesn't fit so well anymore. People then feel they've outgrown the relationship. They might divorce and go their separate ways, or stay together and somehow transform the relationship. Other people find themselves stuck in a worn-out career and go in a new direction. The old skin doesn't fit anymore. We have to let go of the old identity in order to become the new person that we are going to become in the future.

Groups go through this as well. You can see this in the history with empires, nations, and religious organizations. They go through periods of ascendancy and they peak. Then they decline and perhaps die away. Sometimes they're reborn into a new version of themselves. I think BTS is anticipating this as a group. They are reaching a peak and are foreseeing a transformation and a rebirth process. This is going to be quite challenging.

I wrote a book some years ago called *In Mid-Life*. It's about three stages of the transformation process that we call midlife: death, liminality and reintegration. Death means letting go of the old life that is no longer working. Liminality is the uncomfortable in-between state. It is full of uncertainty, and it requires facing the unknown and discovering new aspects of our personality. Finally, reintegration brings a new sense of self to move forward with. This can take a lot of time. The midlife transformation is often five to 10 years in duration.

Now that BTS members have hit incredible heights within their careers, they begin anticipating the trials of transformation. *Map of the Soul: 7* suggests this.

The Songs of *Map of the Soul: 7*

There are two songs that were released on the initial extended play, *Map of the Soul: Persona*, that were left off the official track list for the final album, *Map of the Soul: 7*. I begin the analysis of this album by considering these two songs, *Mikrokosmos* and *Home*, before proceeding to the official track list.

Mikrokosmos

Microcosm is a longstanding idea that humans are a microcosm reflecting the macrocosm. The macrocosm is the cosmos. The cosmos is the totality of everything that is, including yourself. The microcosm is the inner world. The inner world reflects the outer world, the cosmic world. A physical example of this mirroring is how the planets orbiting the sun look just like the electrons orbiting the nuclei of atoms. Similarly, the inner world mirrors the cosmos and vice versa.

Jung stated during a time of illness late in life: "I had a wonderful dream in my illness. I dreamt that I saw a star in a pool of water. And I realized that I am the microcosm reflected in the pool of the unconscious that is the macrocosm. And this gave me a great feeling of well-being." (Jung, *Memories, Dreams, Reflections*, 1989)

If you have a sense of your inner world as microcosm reflecting the outer macrocosm, you have a sense of vast space, complexity, richness and diversity. This is your inner world. It's not all conscious. In fact, much of it is unconscious, but you can have access to it through various techniques that Jungians have developed, methods like active imagination and dream work.

The song *Mikrokosmos* makes frequent reference to the stars. This is an important step in the individuation process. You realize you have an inner self that is connected with the stars and that isn't dependent on others. If you're stuck in persona, you depend on other people reflecting your value and you don't have a sense of self apart from what they give you. Now, with a sense of your inner microcosm reflecting the cosmos, you're linked to a star. You have a sense of worth that comes from within yourself, that's not dependent on the reflections of other people.

So this BTS personality is freeing itself from the persona need to be loved by others and reflected and admired by others. This personality is freeing itself from persona identification and the problems that brings. We each shine in our own way, the song says.

This reminds me of the philosophy of a 17th century German philosopher named Leibniz who had the theory that we're all *monads*. Each of us is an individual self-enclosed monad, but we are in relationship to all the other monads in the universe, all the other people. Every personality is a total individual, but it is in relationship with the other individuals. The song speaks of seven billion stars, which is the population of the world. Each monad is a star. Each one is an individual. Each one has a soul. And yet we're all linked in some mysterious way that Leibniz talked about as "harmony." The monads are harmonized by another force called God, which makes for a harmonious interplay of all the independent pieces, each one having its own center of gravity.

So this is a song about a glimpse of the Self; a glimpse of that feeling that we are deeply rooted in something way beyond ourselves. We're individual, but we also belong to the whole. We have a destiny, that is our individual star, to become ourselves and upon our death to return to that star. That was Gnostic philosophy, which Jung expresses in the *Red Book*. What brings us peace is to know that we have a destiny. That destiny is our star, where we will arrive someday but are linked to it in the meantime. So I read this song's lyrics as a breakthrough into this sense of Self. This personality, represented by these seven young men, is struggling toward a sense of Self and is beginning to find its way.

Home

In the song titled *Home*, BTS uses the Spanish word for my home, mi *Casa*. *Mi Casa* adds a feeling of intimacy. It's a small house. *Mi Casa* is a cottage or a humble dwelling, it's not a palace. The sense of home is also a home with a soul. When you're home with a soul, you're in an intimate space that feels very comfortable, not grandiose or inflated, but grounded and authentic.

RM in his United Nations talk said: "I'm a boy from a small village near Seoul. Now I'm famous. I'm a world celebrity." So you have this feeling of *mi Casa* is back there at home. Their international trips and journeys take them far abroad, and home for them now is everywhere. Their fans are everywhere.

Anywhere you feel loved and accepted can be home, but *mi Casa* is something different. It's more intimate. It's the return. This BTS personality is going out on a long journey, but will come back to where it all began. While it is on the journey it is remembering home. It is like Odysseus wandering for 20 years until he finally got back to Ithaca, to his home and his wife Penelope. While you're gone, you're thinking of *mi Casa*, my home.

The Track List for BTS's Album, *Map of the Soul:* 7

Track 1: *Intro: Persona*

Persona is a Latin word meaning the *mask* that actors wore onstage while they were personifying characters in the play. There is a suggestion of the theatrical whenever you deal with persona. We are all actors on the stage of life, and some of us are a little more theatrical than others. But even withdrawn introverts have a persona when they come out of their shell and face the rest of the world. So the mask, or the persona, is what we have between ourselves and the social world around us.

The way I understand BTS, is that these seven young men represent different aspects of a single personality. We're talking about a single person with different faces. Some of them are a little more serious. Some of them are more entertaining. Some are prettier than others. They have different colored hair. Some smile more than others. So when RM sings the first song, *Persona*, and he asks himself, "who am I," it is a question he says he's had his whole life. We see the other six members dancing around him. They are other aspects. He is the voice, but the others are different facets of the personality. These songs are an expression of a singular personality with different aspects and different personas.

These are songs of longing and struggle for authenticity. One feels this personality is struggling to say something, to come to terms with himself and with who he is and what he is. There are songs of love, hope and vision, as well as despair. There's an intense feeling of being a celebrity and the problems it brings with ego-inflation and self-doubt. There's a search for a place of quiet and truth. It's poignant. I feel empathy for this personality struggling with issues that have arisen in his life by virtue of his great talent and now his fame that doesn't satisfy all of his needs. It satisfies his ambition, but also leaves him feeling empty at times.

He's struggling with a multitude of images of himself, several voices and demands on him to be this or to be that or pressures to change. I imagine these BTS performers really do face those demands as they emerge onto the international scene from their Korean homes and experience all kinds of pressures on them to say this or to do that. It's very tempting, of course, if you have an audience that is expecting a certain kind of performance to give it to them, which BTS can do very well. But when they go home after the show, you wonder how do they feel. That is what is expressed in these songs. There's a lot of introspection and self-evaluation and looking behind their mask. They're making a confession on-stage even while they're entertaining us. That's what makes it so interesting. They are presenting us with a very exciting persona, yet there is something else in the background that they're also singing about.

In *Intro: Persona*, RM sings of hiding his anxiety, which leads him to hesitate. But then he is able to befriend his hesitation. This is a good move, to take your feeling, accept it and not let it stop you, but acknowledge it and hold it.

When he speaks later about when being drunk, he is speaking of immaturity, and how we try to hide this immaturity. It is often a sense of insufficiency or foolishness that we hide at those times. His persona mask makes him feel uneasy as he tries to hide the immaturity that comes with his youth. His lyrics then move into a litany of how he is not good enough.

Many people have a similar sense when they are suddenly thrust into a position that is a bit above where they have been, whether it's in a business position or academic or professional role. They may feel like they're faking, or they're not really up to the position, and so they have to bluff their way through. A lot of professional people have confessed that they feel like fakes. This is like when he sings about hiding his immaturity. He's out there on-stage performing extremely well, and yet he's afraid that it's perhaps more than he can handle.

So that's what the mask is hiding. But then he says: "There's something that raises me up again." What is it that raises him up again? There is a kind of religious sensitivity or sensibility here. That phrase is almost biblical, "He has raised me up again." In Jungian psychology, we would call that the Self. The Self is the core of your being. It's who you were from the day you were born or even before you were born, and is the ultimate resource of the psyche. When you're down, there's this kind of source of energy, inspiration that will raise you up again and give you another chance and a new day. This theme appears in a number of their songs.

Later in this first song he calls out: "Where's your soul?" and "Where's your dream?" He then proclaims: "My name is R," and "I'm not embarrassed anymore. This is the map of my soul."

Track 2: *Boy With Luv*

The first song is about calling out for the soul: "*Where are you?*" In the second song, there is a response; the soul appears.

The soul figure appears as a woman. In the song, an American young lady, *Halsey* (Ashley Frangipane), joins in the vocals. In the beginning of the video for that song, she's in a booth and suddenly realizes she's being called. So she closes up the booth and disappears. You then see the seven BTS members on-stage as they're singing the first part of the song. She joins them later, part way through the song.

Some people have asked why they would choose an American woman to play this role. I found that choice very touching and integrative. They've gone international. They've gone to America to give concerts in Los Angeles, Chicago, and New York. They're reaching out to the international community. But it is also not at all surprising that the soul figure, what we call the Anima figure, is of a culture quite different from their home culture. I think that for Koreans it could be that the American woman is a suitable projection carrier for their Anima. They project their unconscious Anima onto an American woman and find their soul figure there.

Europeans have traditionally projected their soul figures onto exotic cultures, whether in the Middle East, India or China. Wolfgang Pauli, a renowned physicist and friend of Jung, for instance, described his Anima figure as Chinese. He dreamed of her several times. It wasn't that he knew a real Chinese woman that he was in love with, but she represented the unconscious Anima in his personality. So the fact that Halsey is American is significant in that she is the unconscious Anima within the Korean collective that is now responding to the call. In the first song, RM sings "Where's your soul?" In the second song, lo and behold, she appears!

The title of the song is *Boy with Luv*. There's a huge difference between being a *boy with love* and being a *boy in love*. If you're in love, you are possessed by an emotion and a projection of the beloved onto somebody else. You are helpless. Your ego is a slave to that emotion. People do all kinds of crazy things when they're *in love*. If you're *with love*, on the other hand, you're much more in control. You're *with it*. You're not *in it*. You bring it with you. You bring your love to the other whom you are casting your eye upon. This implies a more mature ego. An immature ego will be *head over heels in love*. A more mature, experienced person will be a person *with love*. Being *with love* is a much less manipulative stance. Psychologically, it's a more advanced state.

So I think this personality that the boys represent has advanced considerably from that earlier moment when it was *in love* to now being *with love*. It's a beautiful song with striking lyrics. It celebrates the healthy power of love. It transforms you. It makes you joyful. But it also has its dangers, namely inflation and taking the *wings of Icarus*. They sing: "With the wings of Icarus you gave me, not toward the sun but towards you, let me fly." In Greek mythology, Icarus, flies too close to the sun and the wax on his wings burns up and he crashes. He gets inflated and flies too high. In the song, this personality is progressing. He's elevated and somewhat inflated, but he's not out of control and he's not going to crash. It's a very good sign from an individuation point of view that he's *with love* and that his love is directed toward his beloved and not toward some fantasy that will lead him to crash and burn.

Track 3: *Make It Right*

Make it Right embodies a journey inward to discover one's soul. The song exclaims "I'm singing to find you." Who is the *you* being called for? It's not clear. Is he talking about his girlfriend? I don't think so. Is he talking about the soul that appeared in the second song? Perhaps. Strikingly, though, there is this recurring line in the song: "Coming back to you and doing it better." He's struggling.

Is the soul something inner? Is it something outer? Or is it some combination of both? Our experience in life, especially in the first half of life, as for the BTS members who are in their 20's, is that we discover the Soul in others and through others. When you are in a relationship with a beloved, you are with your soul. That's why it becomes so crucial to be with her. She (or he) is your soul. Inner and outer are mingled through the psychic function of "projection."

The song continues: "It's the answer to my journey. Sing to find you. Baby to you." He may be talking to another person, but he's also talking about his soul and the journey to her. "Sing to find you. Baby to you" is a search for soul. Maybe he's looking outward, but it's also a journey inward at the same time. This is a wonderful song about the journey to find the Soul.

He sings: "I remember the night sky I saw in my childhood," again a reference to the stars. There's a wonderful poem titled "My Name" by the American poet Mark Strand, who speaks about lying in a field at night looking up at the stars and suddenly hearing his name called. He says he's never heard his name called like that. Looking at the stars and hearing your name called is a moment of initiation and transformation. When you hear your name called in that way, or your beloved calls your name, it's a different calling. "Make it Right" suggests that the singer is coming to himself. It's profoundly moving.

Track 4: *Jamais Vu*

Continuing with the international theme, Song 4 is titled *Jamais Vu*. *Jamais vu* is a French phrase that is actually a psychiatric term for a psychological disorder. Linguistically, it's related to *déjà vu*. If you have a *déjà vu* experience, you have an intense feeling of "I've been here before," despite being in a new location that you haven't seen before. You usually can't say when or where it was that you were there before, but the feeling is present nonetheless. You might even know what a person is going to say next, and lo and behold they say it. It's like you've been in this film before. That's *déjà vu*.

Jamais vu is the opposite. This describes the experience that you're in a familiar place, but you don't recognize it. It's a weird and disorienting moment. People with temporal lobe epilepsy and occasionally schizophrenia can have this problem. You might walk into your own home, but you don't recognize it, like you've never been there before. You have to learn the place all over again.

This song is about repetitions and repeating, like you don't learn from experience. Every time you face the same problem, you have to learn about it all over again. You make the same mistakes over and over. In Jungian psychology we attribute such episodes of repeatedly struggling with the same issues to a *complex*.

When you are caught up in a complex, you step into the same situation and react the same way over and over a again as though you haven't learned anything from your past experiences. Each episode is usually hurtful to others or harmful to yourself, leading to regret for what you've said or done. You repeat the same patterns, even though in your head you may well know where it's going to lead. Yet it's like a brand new situation every time. You had the same argument with your partner last night, and now you have it again like you hadn't had it before. Don't you learn? No. The complex is too strong. The pattern just runs itself over and over until you can somehow break out of it through an insight or intervention. The song proclaims "It always hurts like it's the first time." This is the product of a complex in action.

The song goes on. "I stumble again. I continue running and I stumble again." But what I found very encouraging was that while all this repetition goes on, there is awareness that is developing at the same time, and at the end of the song the last line he asserts: "I won't give up." There is a determination to stay on the path of individuation even though you fall off many times and you repeat your old mistakes and unproductive behaviors.

In psychotherapy, we know that going over and over repeated difficult feelings and behaviors allows you to recognize them and reduces their severity. Maybe it takes you less time to recover from the emotions. Maybe you see through it sooner rather than later. Maybe you can name the complex. Even while you're in it, you can perhaps say to yourself: "Oh my God, why am I doing this?" and kind of pull yourself out. It is very hard to do. That's the struggle of fighting with our complexes for the sake of individuation.

I've worked with some people in therapy for over 30 years. They say to me, "You know, we've gone over this ground a hundred times, and I did it again." We may laugh about it. But we never quite get over it totally. We get better at it, but we have to recognize that psychological life is a struggle. Becoming conscious and staying conscious is incredibly difficult.

Track 5: *Dionysus*

This is a song of celebration and breaking out of the persona. Dionysus was a foreign god to the Greeks. He came down from Thrace and invaded Greece. Dionysus is a disruptor, he upsets everything. He tramples on old values. He breaks down people's resistance. You can't resist Dionysus when he comes. If you try, he will overwhelm you.

So this is a song of how this personality BTS has gotten to the place of Dionysian celebration. They aren't afraid of Dionysus. They can accept him, and they can enjoy his intoxication. They're breaking down barriers and old habits. Dionysus was called the loosener. The loosener dissolves old structures, rigid behaviors and patterns, and destroys personas.

He frees you of your persona... at least momentarily. Of course, you might wake up the next morning and wish he hadn't. The intoxication can be too much, can get out of hand and become destructive.

In the end, the Greeks were able integrate Dionysus into their Pantheon. They gave him a place at Delphi where the sacred oracle held forth upon request. Apollo, who was the classic god of the Greeks - a god of order, beauty, structure, healing, high mindedness and nobility - had to share his temple at Delphi half of the year with Dionysus. The ancient Greek culture was able to integrate Dionysus into their collective psyche because they recognized that you can't resist him. He is the life force. If you resist him, he will break you.

Some respond to the call of Dionysus by attempting to stay as upright and perfect as possible. They become rigid in their social correctness. Their personas are fixed and inflexible. This is very dangerous. You can't safely just repress this aspect of the unconscious and its powers. You may try to ignore Dionysus but he will find you. You've got to find another way to let him live in your life. If you try to restrain him too much, he will break out with unbridled intensity.

In Swiss culture, they have a day called *Fasnacht*, and it's the equivalent of Mardi Gras in other countries. It's the beginning of Lent. Lent is a very serious time in the calendar of Christian culture, but at the beginning the Swiss have a day called Fasnacht, when people dress up in masks, stay out all night and do all kinds of crazy things that they would not normally indulge in. The rule is that the next day you cannot speak about it. You cannot confront somebody and say, "Oh, I saw you behaving like a beast last night." It's a night of freedom. Jung described *Fasnacht* as a safety valve to *let the steam out of the kettle*. Otherwise, the Swiss, being rather upright and conventional, compulsive about order and correct behavior, would explode. Human beings need the release that Dionysus allows.

For BTS to celebrate Dionysus the way they do suggests they are ready to let go of persona and break out of the traps persona sets. They are arriving at a point of release from the constraints of the persona.

Track 6: *Interlude: Shadow*

Whenever we touch the shadow in ourselves or others, emotion rushes in. Throughout the song *Interlude: Shadow*, we feel this emotional intensity in Suga's passionate desire for fame, power, and fortune as well as his fear and anxiety. In the film, there are images of shattering glass and mirrors. Looking in the mirror and confronting your shadow is bound to be a *shattering* experience. It destroys self-images and constructed images of the surrounding world. It breaks your self-confidence and destroys your naiveté. This can, of course, prepare the ground for a new consciousness, but in the meantime it's a harrowing experience.

What is the shadow? It's a carefully concealed part of the psyche that clings to the backside of the ego. It sits there in obscurity, moving quietly and unobtrusively in the background as you go about your daily affairs. Some parts of the shadow lie just at the fringe of consciousness, and you can sense them occasionally out of the corner of your eye. But mostly the shadow is not apparent to the ego. Sometimes, though, you might stop and take a deeper look within and see that behind your persona and your ego-consciousness there lurks a dark figure, which we speak of as the shadow.

If you are courageous, you can admit it into consciousness. You can let it speak to you, and then you can catch aspects of it lying there at the fringe of consciousness. Suga sings, as though to himself, "I want to be a rap star, I want to be the top, I want to be a rock star, I want it all mine." He is letting the shadow take his voice and speak through him, showing its usually hidden features. Suga is telling us his most passionate wishes and desires. It's as though he is speaking to himself in private and letting us listen in on his internal dialogue. The most hidden part of ourselves is our coldest egotism, our most profoundly selfish part. When we face it, it can be a truly shattering experience.

Of course, we have the capacity to love as well as to hate, a capacity for altruism and a capacity for selfishness. BTS sings frequently and beautifully about love: Being in love, being with love, loving ourselves, and loving those around us. But in this album, BTS is singing about the dark side, the shadow. The shadow is the other side of love. It houses our greed and ambition and lust for power over others, as Suga sings so well. Whereas love reaches out to others and wants their good, the shadow withdraws into egotism and wants to use others for its own benefit and to control them for selfish purposes. Our ego can lean either way. It can be taken up by the light or by the dark.

Interlude: Shadow is about becoming conscious of the shadow in an honest and straightforward way. Suga becomes aware of his shadow desires, and he opens a dialogue with them. In the last part of the piece, there's a conversation between Suga and his shadow. The shadow tells him that they are one and that they can never be separated.

Dialogue was also how Jung engaged the shadow in his famous *Red Book*. There we can read his dialogues with all sorts of light and dark figures, including the Devil himself. This is a way of becoming familiar with those parts of the self. By imaging them and entering into a conversational relationship with them, a person allows them not only to become more familiar but also drains some of the energy from them.

In the video version of *Interlude: Shadow*, Suga emerges from a door with a bright red surround. Red is the color of very strong emotional energy, the color of passion, sometimes of anger, sometimes of lust. We don't know what is behind the door, but I imagine it's a house of darkness. He is coming out into consciousness and is going to reveal what he knows. He is alone. Down the hallway are a number of men also standing alone in front of other doors, each one isolated and showing no relationship to each other. Suga will be the solo performer in this song. It's all about the isolated individual, alone, outside of relationship to the others who happen to be around him. Suga stands for the BTS group's shadow, isolated from the world around.

Suga sings, "I wanna be rich, I wanna be the king, I want it all mine, I wanna be me, I want a big thing, I want it all mine ..." This is the shadow of greed speaking through the ego. And then, suddenly, he has a moment of recognition of his dangerous situation, and he falls into terrible anxiety. Now he suddenly experiences the harsh reality of the opposites: Intense light begets intense darkness. The brighter the light, the darker the dark. The higher he rises above everyone, the farther is the ground below him. Suga fears falling, which is the inevitable result of overreaching and flying too high too fast. He sings: "The moment I'm flying high as I wished, my shadow grows in that blasting stark light. Please don't let me shine. Don't let me down. Don't let me fly. Now I'm afraid." He's praying for deliverance from the consequences of his shadow enactments. He's speaking for BTS: Great success breeds great anxiety. The richer you become, the more you fear poverty.

Many people fear the consequences of too much success gained too soon. It's an instinctual fear, and it makes sense. Success breeds envy in others, and in their envy, they will plot the demise of the successful one. Think of Iago in Shakespeare's masterpiece of evil, *Othello*. Or recall the famous cautionary tale from Greek mythology, the story of Icarus. Icarus and his father, Daedalus, were trapped in a labyrinth. Daedalus, a skilled craftsman, builds them each a set of wings so they can fly out. The father ascends to a moderate height and lands safely outside. Icarus, on the other hand, becomes thrilled with his power to fly. He flaps his wings too hard and flies too high, whereupon the sun melts the wax holding his wings to his naked arms, and he crashes to his death. The fear of flying too high too fast is not a bad thing. It's a useful anxiety. We have these anxieties for a reason.

Toward the end of the song we hear a voice singing: "I'm you, you're me, now do you know? Yeah you are me, I'm you, now you do know." Who is singing these words? It's Suga's alter ego, his shadow. The song has shifted from monologue to dialogue. His shadow is speaking to him, and it's telling him a truth. It is the shadow speaking to Suga saying: "We are one, do you get it? You can't get rid of me. We are connected. We will always be together. We are one body, and we are going to clash, you are me ... do you know this?" This forecasts a new consciousness and an acceptance of the shadow. The shadow will always be there, and it's better to accept this truth than to deny it and try to repress the shadow into the unconscious where you can't see it.

What we get in this song is a picture of ambition and success. It's a message that says when you're in the world and working hard, you want to rise. But ambition also activates the shadow side of ego striving upward. One makes decisions that are selfish in a hidden way, perhaps putting yourself ahead of somebody else, or stabbing them quietly in the back, or doing things that are not quite correct or are even illegal or unethical. We do these things semiconsciously or totally unconsciously. One can't avoid it. The song of Suga shows a deep recognition that we can't get away from the shadow. Nobody is free of the shadow.

There is also a collective side to shadow. We project our personal and the collective shadow onto the marginalized people in society, onto criminals, refugees, immigrants, and people of a different nationality or race. They are the shadow-bearers of society. But this projection denies the deep bond of kinship that actually exists among all of us as human beings. Suga ends his song with: "We are one body and we are gonna clash. We are you, we are me, this do you know?" He is affirming our commonality and ultimate oneness. We are all related.

Track 7: *Black Swan*

Black Swan explores despair, the dreadful disappearance of meaning. The song was first released via a video of a professional dance company performing to BTS's *Black Swan*. The video opens with a quote from Martha Graham: "A dancer dies twice—once when they stop dancing, and this first death is the more painful."

A dancer often lives for dancing, and dancing can become the essential meaning of their life. Dancers, like the BTS performers, put everything into their work, into their professional vocation. When dancers' bodies give out, which often happens relatively early in their lives, their life's meaning can suddenly evaporate. BTS is anticipating this moment, when the group will inevitably fall apart and the members will stop performing. This will be their first death and the most painful of deaths. The second death, of course, will be their physical death. The song is a realization that all things will end. One's successful moments in the spotlight will come to an end. The lights will go out, and you'll be alone, you'll be without the audience, without the applause. It's a very difficult feeling to come to terms with. We feel the anguish in this song.

In the *Black Swan* video, you can see the struggles of the white swan trying to fly and the black ones surrounding it and holding it back. It's moving but without success because it can't fly, and it's being crushed by the black swans surrounding it. That's how moods affect us when we fall into a depression or our life loses its meaning. This can happen to anybody and in many different ways. A loved one dies, or you have an accident and you can't do anymore what you could before, you have a stroke, you lose your job. There are many ways you can experience that moment in life. It's not the end of life, though. Those ballet dancers can find another career, perhaps teaching ballet or writing a book about ballet or doing something else in relation to it.

But it is a moment of darkness that is very challenging to overcome. The resilient ego can cope with it and move on.

Track 8: *Filter*

Filter is Jimin's solo song, and he asks: "Which of me do you want?" BTS is an entertainment group, and they can cheer you up, excite you or calm you down. This filter idea is "I can be anything you want, just tell me what you want, I'll be it." It's not the way relationships work in the long run, but it's a phase perhaps, and it's certainly what entertainment tries to do. For a period of time, it will make you feel something outside your normal frame of reference. BTS is saying, "We can do that. We can dance for you. We can help you." They're great entertainers and engage with the audience extraordinarily well.

It can also be speaking of a bias towards one of the seven in the group. Which one of the seven are we perhaps most drawn to? "Which of me do you want?" could also mean which one of the BTS members do you want? It could be the one you're attracted to the most, or the one you can identify with the most. It could also be the one you project a part of yourself onto the most and thus feel closest to.

You have seven BTS members moving around, and it's hard to keep them apart unless you focus on one or two. One of the functions of consciousness is to differentiate. So, when you see a group, you begin trying to separate them and distinguish them. This one does this better, that one does that better. I like this one better than that one. It's a normal part of conscious functioning to do that. That's how we develop one-sidedness and bias, by making selections and preferences. I like RM because he speaks English and I can understand him better, and he made such a good talk at the United Nations. So, I would tend to favor him, but I'm also drawn to the group as a whole.

Track 9: *My Time*

In *My Time*, Jungkook sings, "It feels as if I became an adult quicker than anyone, and there are traces of what I missed. Am I living this right?" He mentions how his friends are on a subway while he's in an airplane. It's something that one hears a lot from celebrities who became famous when they were young. They feel as if they've missed out on their childhood and adolescence. The BTS members were enlisted into the group at an early age. Their lives became suddenly intense and very fast moving and highly disciplined, and they missed out on a lot of usual teenage experiences. It's as if they were put in a chute or a tunnel, and shot through and didn't see what's outside that framework. So, when they're in their 20's, as they are now, and they look back, they see how narrow that tunnel was and think of all the experiences they missed.

Another theme in these songs is the awareness of time. As you grow out of childhood, you begin realizing that the passage of time is irreversible. That's a part of growing into adulthood. We often notice that adolescents seem to have a feeling of invulnerability and immortality. "Choices don't really matter; I can always start over again." People usually outgrow that adolescent attitude in their early 20s. Then you realize that the choices you've made are significant and they have consequences, and you can't go back and start all over again. You get the sense in some of these songs that time is being registered in a new way. That's a part of ego development. Time becomes more and more important, and you start measuring time differently and more precisely. You start relating to a clock differently because you realize you have deadlines and a shrinking amount of time available.

Ultimately, it's about moving toward a midlife crisis when death anxiety typically sets in. It dawns on people that it's not just others who are going to die; you are going to die as well. Time is passing, and you can't recapture it. There is no returning to childhood.

Track 10: *Louder than Bombs*

Louder than Bombs is a statement of empathy. BTS is looking outside their own suffering and toward that of the wider world. They're seeing the suffering of migrants, the suffering of people who are the victims of climate change, or warfare, or pandemics. There is so much suffering in the world, and it seeps into us and we feel it. BTS is showing their empathy to the suffering of others in the world, including their ARMY of fans. "We feel with you; we know some of you are in really hard places." They are reaching out in solidarity with the suffering of the outside world. They're saying: BTS cares! We feel your pain! This is a sign of maturity.

Track 11: *ON*

Jung once said, "Send me a sane man, and I will cure him." Sanity is a highly valued virtue and quality. We all want to be sane, we want our family members to be sane, we want our society to be sane, but sanity by itself isn't enough. It lacks imagination. It lacks depth. It's basically just common sense, and while we need it and it's valuable, it doesn't nearly satisfy the needs of the psyche for meaning and creativity and imagination. A "sane person" is someone who is not in touch with the unconscious. That's what Jung meant: I will take that sane person and put them in contact with the unconscious. That will give them depth. Wholeness is not based only on rational consciousness.

Jung's path to wholeness was to contact the unconscious through working with dreams, active imagination and other methods, so that you can be in touch with other parts of yourself that we would call, not necessarily insane, but irrational and off the beaten track. That's where your creativity will be. That's where your life energy will come from.

"ON" is also very much about resilience, about overcoming difficulties and going on. BTS shows a quality that is described in the theory called "anti-fragility." Anti-fragility is a quality that some things have that allows them to survive severe shocks and traumas. If an object is anti-fragile, it can fall on a hard surface from a height and not break. Fragile things like glasses and vases break. Your cell phone has been made to be anti-fragile. You can drop it, it can fall in the toilet, it can crash to the ground, and it usually doesn't break or become nonfunctional. It's anti-fragile. That's what we strive for when we work with people in psychotherapy - to make them anti-fragile. We're all going to take hits, blows, setbacks, discouraging times, failures, etc. It's inevitable, and if you're fragile they will break you. To make some-body anti-fragile is to make them resilient so they can bounce back. They can fall, be hurt emotionally and suffer the pain, and yet they can pick themselves up and go on. That's what this song is about. Keep on moving, keep on going, no matter how bad the times get.

Track 12: *Ugh!*

The song *Ugh!* expresses disgust at people who hide behind masks and direct their anger against others anonymously. It urges people to take a stand against a world dominated by rage. And it gives a glimpse into the pain BTS must have felt as targets of such disguised anger. Trolls and bullies fill all corners of the Internet and social media. You might get a smile when a person sees you, but then that same person bullies you on Facebook. Posts on Twitter and other platforms routinely draw large numbers of bullying "trolls" if the post is at all controversial. A lot of that anger comes from envy, jealousy, and projection. BTS must get a lot of that. The envy must be enormous from the other K-pop groups and other people who've not been as successful as they've been. I'm sure they take a lot of hits. It can really take a toll: *Ugh!*

Track 13: *Zero O'Clock*

Zero O'Clock is the midnight hour. It's when the old day ends and a new one begins. This is a song about endings and new beginnings. It's a rebirth song. It's related to Track 9, *My Time*, with the theme of recognition that time marches on. As one leaves childhood and enters adulthood, time takes on new meaning. And one also realizes that there are cycles in time: All things end, and all endings are followed by rebirth into something new. At zero o'clock, aka midnight, one is at the turning point of that transition.

Track 14: *Inner Child*

Inner Child, is sung by V. It's his solo song, and it's fitting that this song is performed by a single voice. It is an intimate account of memories of childhood. This is a song of nostalgia, a tender remembering of experiences from days gone by and wrapped in the warm blanket of maternal nurturance and protection.

The "inner child" is also often related in psychological writings to experiences of trauma in childhood. This phrase became extensively used in studies of early trauma. Donald Kalsched is one of the most significant Jungians to take up the theme of trauma and of how children defend themselves against it. The child has a trauma and then elaborates a defense system that can be both protective and destructive. Kalsched has a wonderful appreciation for the spirit that the child is protecting, its divine essence. The protective shield that develops is a double-edged sword, because on the one hand it does keep the trauma out in a way, but it also keeps the child separated from life and later the adult separated from life as well.

The song, *Inner Child*, is also symbolic. The references include memories of childhood, but they also extend out much further in meaning for the present and future. The inner child is not only the child of the past but also the child of the present and the potential for the future. It's an archetype. It's the part of you that's new, has a futuristic orientation, can grow, can develop. The inner child can be very sensitive, as children often are, but it also has great potential. When we speak of the inner child in psychology, we're speaking of a person's potential for future growth and development as well as of memories of childhood.

Track 15: *Friends*

Friends is a duet between Jimin and V. Throughout the song, they sing, "Stay here, stay by my side." They've been friends since their school days, and they remain dear to one another. The song is also anticipating an inevitable, at least partial, separation. *Map of the Soul: 7* is as a whole about the completion of an opus, of a large body of work. The album is announcing this completion and therefore implying an ending. This is implicit in the album even if it is very noticeable in many of the songs. This album announces the ending of a period or a phase. In the face of this realization, Jimin and V affirm their long friendship, which is precious to them. True friendship between men is something very rare in our world. When friendships are formed at an early age, they have the potential to last for a lifetime. But people's lives take unexpected twists and turns, and friends go in different directions. People grow and change, like snakes who shed their skins, and this may mean they move apart from another. This is something to grieve because it's a loss. But deep friendships can be enduring. *Friends* honors this connection.

Track 16: *Moon*

Moon is sung by Jin. It's his solo song. He takes the role of the Moon singing to the Earth, which is the ARMY of BTS fans around the world. It's significant that BTS uses the moon to symbolize the light shining out to the fans. The moon is a light in the darkness. It's very dramatic visually, very romantic. However, the moon, unlike the sun, is changeable. It goes through phases. Sometimes it's bright, sometimes it's very dim. The song suggests cycles when BTS is sometimes shining brightly and at other times dimly. It's a kind of love song.

Track 17: *Respect*

One of the most frequently cited reasons people give for committing violent acts is that they felt "dissed," that is, *disrespected* in some way. Disrespect feels like humiliation and triggers violent outbursts leading to catastrophic acts. Disrespect enrages many people. Disrespect is a very important feature in domestic violence. When children don't respect their parents, or parents don't respect their children, or spouses don't respect each other, violent arguments erupt that can lead to violent acts.

In this song, BTS sings of respect as the highest and most difficult virtue to achieve. They sing, it's easy *to say* you respect another person, but to follow through and behave accordingly is another matter. Acting with respect is the critical test. "*Re-spect* means as it sounds, to literally look again and again, Look again and again and you'll see faults, But you still want to keep looking, despite of that." They're urging us to keep looking at the other. When you keep looking at someone, you're bound to see their flaws, but the fact that you nonetheless want to keep looking and, I would add, looking without judgment, shows that you respect them.

Track 18: *We Are Bulletproof: The Eternal*

In *We Are Bulletproof: The Eternal*, BTS sings together. "We were only seven, but we have you all now. We're not afraid anymore, together we are bulletproof." It's an affirmation that they and ARMY are one, and together they are invulnerable to the slings and arrows of hate and criticism. They're bulletproof, they won't go down. They even claim immortality. To say that they are *eternal* is a very big statement indeed. It's saying they have overcome time itself. Temporality does not affect them, and many years from now, even after they are dead and gone, they will still be present, and their music will still be inspiring young people. They are putting BTS up there among the stars that never change. It's a very strong claim, and it's also affirming the strength of their unity as a group and of their unity with ARMY fans.

Track 19: *Outro : Ego*

Outro is typically a concluding section of music, but we don't really know what *outro* means in this song. Does it mean it's the end of the whole series or is it the concluding song of this album? What does this song mean in the lives of BTS? What are they saying about themselves? As mentioned before, I look upon BTS as a single personality. Even though the songs are sung by individuals, like J-Hope and Suga and so on, they're still singing for the group as a whole. Now BTS is getting older. They started as a boys group, but they aren't boys anymore. The K-pop groups are usually very young adolescents, teenagers, but these BTS performers are now in their mid-20s. They're reaching another stage of life and they're becoming mature adults. Before too long they'll be in their 30's.

Outro: Ego celebrates the moment when we realize "I am I." I am not you; I am not some other through identification with them. No, I am I. Jung had this experience and records it in his auto-biography, *Memories, Dreams, Reflections*. He said it was like stepping out of a cloud, and suddenly he realized: I am I, I am myself. This coming to oneself and affirming one's uniqueness, one's individuality, is the coming of age of the ego. It is an initiation into life as an individual, separate from others. "I am" means "I exist as an I," as one of a kind. The sense of temporality is a strong part of this song; it is the sense of time passing. I'm here for only a short period of time in the history of the world. This is ego awareness, the reality of time and finitude. This song is an *outro* in the sense of BTS finishing one stage of life and taking up the next. This is all part of the individuation of the members of BTS and of BTS as a group.

Individuation is the term that Jung used to describe psychological development through the entire span of life from the months spent in the mother's womb until the last breath is given up and the person passes away. That is the lifespan of the individual. What happens psychologically and developmentally within that lifespan is what Jung called individuation. Individuation ultimately means becoming the individual that you are born to be. You are born with a certain code - a genetic code, but also a psychological code - that underlies the emergence of your potentials and development of talents and abilities.

In *Outro: Ego,* J-Hope sings that "time rushes ever forward" and about "choices by my fate." He speaks of memories of when he was a child, and in the video there's a photograph of him as a little boy. This has to do with the realization that the important decisions we make in life determine our life's course with some finality. When you're young, you think, well, there are so many different directions you could take, so many things you could do. Maybe you'll try one thing for a while, and if it doesn't work out you'll try something else for a while. The consequences of choices are minimized. When you're young, there are vast potentials, and you don't have to settle on anything in particular right away. For BTS members, however, their fate was sealed when they were identified as having an amazing musical performance ability and were taken into training. The decision to go along with that opportunity, whoever made the decision, became their fate and their destiny. That is their life, and it's irreversible. When you get the sense that time flows in only one direction and that is forward, and you also realize it doesn't go backward or stand still, then you're living in the ego. Ego lives with temporality, with the flow of time from past to present to future, one way.

Before the ego is very well developed, time doesn't exist in the same sense. For the infant, time is not a factor; it lives in atemporality, the eternal Now. This is a paradisal state: No time, no death, no aging, no yesterday or tomorrow. As you grow older, you begin to live with a sense of temporality, and you learn to take time seriously into account as you make your decisions. You live in process and in a con-sequential world where decisions make a difference, and there are hard decisions and roads not taken. You cannot return to the past. J-Hope remembers his childhood, and there's nostalgia in the memory. Of course, it's important to remember the past, but you cannot go back. The realization that you can't go backward into the past and that time does not stand still but moves ever forward is a very important moment. Suddenly, you realize that you have to face the present and the future. The choices we make have effects not only in the moment but for the future.

J-Hope is coming to that realization in the song. He sings, "touch of the devil, fateful recall." The devil is shadow, and perhaps a devil was involved in his decision to become a BTS star, the devil of ambition. In the earlier song in the album, *Interlude: Shadow*, Suga sings: "I wanna be a Rockstar" and "I wanna be rich." There is the touch of the devil in some of the choices we make; that is, the shadow gets in and pushes us in a certain direction, motivates us to take a certain step, and then we come to the realization that we can't reverse this process that has been set in motion. We look back and we may think, "Wow, I wonder if I really should have done that. Maybe I shouldn't have." But it's too late, and you can't undo it. You can't redo the past; it is done. You have to move forward and grieve the past, or remember it and honor it, but you cannot go back into it.

Later in *Outro: Ego*, J-Hope's face is super-imposed on paintings of ancient gods. There can be a danger of inflation, since one's celebrity status can feel godlike. When the ego comes into this level of fame and is able to celebrate itself, it can appear godlike to itself and to others. It's a dangerous moment because the ego can exaggerate its capacities and its ability to control life and events. Besides, it's not real and will eventually prove to be empty, another mask. The gods are imagined by human beings to live a more or less pain-free life. In most pantheons, the gods are beyond human suffering and beyond the effects of time. They create and they destroy. They have control of time itself. They're very different from the way we experience our lives here in the body. The Greeks talked about hubris, and when humans start thinking that they are gods, they're running the risk of being punished by the gods and struck down. This may come in the form of an illness, an accident, some kind of dire misfortune. In an earlier song, *Interlude: Shadow*, Suga is begging not to fly too high because there's a clear realization that the young person who flies too high will get burned by the sun, will collapse, and will fall to his death. In the song, there's an anxiety about inflation. In *Outro: Ego*, however, the experience of success in the ego is more affirmative. This is a moment in the album of affirming the ego, which can be a beautiful thing. It's in line with the way Jung felt about the ego: The ego is not a bad thing. The ego is our consciousness, it's our awareness, and it's very wrapped up with our individuality. We can affirm the ego. It's a good thing to have a strong ego, just not one that's too inflated.

I think BTS is closing their album with the affirmation, "Yes, we have arrived at this stage of consciousness." The album starts with *Persona*, then moves through *Shadow*, and ends with *Ego*. This is not without meaning. This is a carefully structured, well-built album. The songs open at the surface of the psyche and then moved inward. They experience the shadow, and they end up with a strong ego. This is an important psychological development. The ego gets strengthened by dealing with and integrating the shadow.

Chapter 3

A Review of the *Map of the Soul*

By Steven Buser and Leonard Cruz

The Map

This map of the soul has two center points, the *ego* and the *archetypal Self*. The *archetypal Self* lies at the core of our *ego*. Because this idea is difficult to depict, we have represented it as a cone through which the *ego* funnels into the *archetypal* Self. We will talk more of these structures shortly.

In the upper righthand corner of the map appears a large eye that looks out toward a village or, more accurately, gazes out to the entire world, taking in the totality of what we physically see, hear, smell, and touch. *Ego* perceives reality through the senses.

Animus

Anima

External World

Persona

Persona

Shadow

Ego

Archetypal Self

C
A

C
A

C
A

C
A

Complex

C
A

Archetypal Core of Complex

Primordial Fire
(deep within collective Unconscious)

Illustration by Steven Buser

The eye sits atop a range of mountains representing the *persona*. The *persona* is located between the *ego* and the surrounding world since it mediates our presentation to the outside world. Most of the world does not see what lies beyond the *persona*, just as a tall mountain range blocks our view of what is beyond. *Persona* is the *mask* we show those around us.

To the far left side of the mountains lies the *shadow* with the *ego* lying midway between. *Shadow* is depicted as a hooded figure. It is no accident that it is found directly opposite to the *persona* on the other side of the mountain range (from the perspective of the *ego*). The *shadow* is the opposite of the *persona*. Whatever positive, acceptable face we show the world through our *persona* is balanced by a darker, unacknowledged, and opposite figure that forms our *shadow*. The *shadow* carries all the unwanted, shameful, unacceptable parts of our psyche. We bury them deep within, hoping they won't be discovered. The *shadow* exists in the unconscious.

In the upper left side of the map, a region that is still in the unconscious realm lie the *anima* and *animus*. These are opposite-gendered, unconscious figures in our soul. The masculine figure is depicted as a warrior, while the feminine figure is dressed in full-length chiton, a type of tunic. The classical Jungian view is that a man possesses a feminine *anima* connecting him to the deeper levels of his unconscious, while a woman possesses a masculine *animus* connecting her to the depths of her unconscious.

Scattered throughout the unconscious lie numerous ovals with a "C" for *complexes* in the middle and a funnel tapering down to a letter "*A*" for *archetype*, which is at the core of a complex. We will explain these later.

Finally, at the bottom of this map are found the flames of the *primordial fire*. This image reminds us that the collective unconscious underlies the entirety of the map. It is here where primitive forces dwell and potent symbols, fears, and inspirations gradually emerge.

The External World

The external world is the easiest part of the map to understand. It represents everything we know as our world. It is everything we can touch, see, and hear and everything present in the physical world with which we interact, including people, objects, and other creatures. The external world contrasts with our internal experience. Our internal experience is harder to grasp and understand, particularly the unconscious realm of which we are not usually aware.

The Ego

The *ego* rests on the surface of the unconscious and occupies the center of consciousness. It is the "I" who speaks, and it is what *I* am aware of when *I* contemplate myself. It lies on the boundary between what we know and what we don't know. It is what we understand consciously of our experience of being human. It acts and sets projects in motion, while encompassing all the traits and characteristics by which we consciously "know ourselves." It is informed and affected by all our memories, traumas, emotions, and facts as well as everything we can consciously sense in our bodies. When we have a "flash of insight," it is often the awareness of something unconscious breaking though to our conscious *ego* awareness.

The Persona

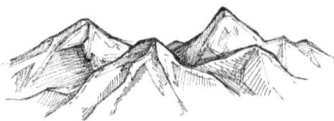

The *persona*, the mountain range, separates our conscious *ego* from the external world and interacts with it. The eye between the *ego* and the external world emphasizes the fact that we look out to the world from our *ego*'s perspective. It is through our senses that we perceive the world around us, and this is represented by the eye looking out. What the world sees as it looks back at us is our *persona*. Thus, in this map, when friends, family, or really anyone looks at us and forms an opinion of us, they are not looking inside our *ego*, but rather at the *persona*, the mask we allow them to see. They see *persona*; they never see the "true us," only the part of ourselves that the *persona* allows them to see. Our *persona* varies, depending on what role we are in. At work, I might be a doctor. Perhaps I dress the part of a doctor by wearing a white coat or other professional clothes. I use language common to physicians, "doctor talk." I sound professional and may even find myself using big words and professional jargon that reinforces my identity and perhaps convinces me and others of my standing. My work *persona* allows me to function more freely and smoothly in my role. When I go home at night, however, if I were to forget to take off my "doctor *persona*" and not put on my "spouse *persona*," bad things will happen. I might order my spouse around, use wordy or professional jargon, insist on things being done my way, etc. At home, the aspects of my *persona* identified with my doctor *persona* are no longer adaptive; it is actually mal-adaptive. At home, I had better put on my "spouse *persona*" or my "father *persona*." With these *personas*, I am less professional; I am more likely to laugh, joke and roll around on the floor with my children. We put on a vast array of *personas* in the course of our lives, including student, friend, mentor, mentee, athlete, partygoer, rock star, social activist, etc.

The *Shadow*

Our *shadow* is the contrary image of our *persona*, its opposite. For every aspect of how we try to present ourselves to the world through our *persona*, an opposite part of our personality gets split off and stored in the *shadow*. If I have worked to make my *persona* come across as a friendly, helpful, and encouraging person, that means that the opposite of those traits, an unfriendly, unhelpful, discouraging person, becomes split off and deposited in my unconscious *shadow*. The intensity of this phenomenon appears to vary in direct proportion with how intense and one-sided my *persona* becomes. A person who presents his or her *persona* to others as an extremely righteous, pious and devoted person lacking any anger or negativity is likely creating an unconscious *shadow* with powerful, cruel, immoral, and irreverent qualities. When the *shadow* makes its presence known, it can be very energetic and forceful in the way it expresses the opposite characteristics. The news has been full of pious preachers speaking out intensely against behaviors they regard as sinful, only to find themselves scandalously caught in those very same actions. One explanation of this is that the more pious their *persona* becomes, the more energized and immoral their *shadow* becomes. Often it is only a matter of time before the unacceptable *shadow* will erupt and become exposed to the public. This sort of *reversal* can be shocking, but it can also be the beginning of a new and more authentic life if handled properly.

Typically, unless we have done a lot of personal work on ourselves, the contents of our *shadow* are hidden and unknown to us. The less we understand about our *shadow* side, the more likely we are to unknowingly act from it, often in ways that hurt others. It is crucial for us to recognize we have a *shadow* side and take steps to deal with it in healthy ways. This consists mostly of becoming conscious of aspects of *shadow* through paying attention to our dreams, to what we find objectionable in others, to what we envy, and by exploring the moments of *reversals* when the *shadow* erupts.

Anima and Animus

Buried within our un-conscious lies another figure that holds the neglected sides of our masculinity or femininity. One hundred years ago, as Carl Jung was developing these theories, gender was more rigidly defined within society. It was seldom tolerated in the Victorian Age for men to show much of their feminine side or vice versa. Thus, a man who went through life embodying mostly masculine qualities remained unaware of an undeveloped and un-conscious feminine figure in his psyche that Jung called the *anima*. It is through the *anima* that a man is able to connect with his softer, more soulful, and perhaps more creative side. When he tears up, swells with intense emotions, or is more driven by the heart than the head, he is likely connecting to his *anima*. This *anima* might come to him in dreams as a sensual or soulful woman. She is his guide to this deeper place within his personality. She is pregnant with new life, heralding the future.

Traditionally, women had the opposite deve-lopment challenge to their identity. They were discouraged from pursuing demanding, male-domi-nated careers and rarely pursued public roles of power and authority. An unconscious masculine figure typically lived hidden away in their un-conscious, a personality with strength, determination, and warrior-like power that Jung called the *animus*. In dreams, this figure often comes to women as a powerful male figure.

In the second half of a woman's life, she might distance herself from an overly nurturing role and develop a second career with a stronger, more forceful, and public personality. At such times, her *animus* is surfacing.

This paradigm has shifted dramatically over the last few decades as gender became more fluid within individuals and society in general. Men are no longer forced into solely masculine expressions of their personality, just as women are allowed more freedom of expression. Nonetheless, whatever gender elements we incline toward, the opposite gender develops unconscious power within our *anima/animus*. Connecting to those opposite gender traits allows us to become more whole and complete.

Complexes

Scattered throughout the unconscious zone of our map are numerous *complexes*. We have symbolized them as a "C" within an oval that funnels down toward the letter "*A*." Each one of us has countless *complexes* within our unconscious.

A *complex* is a sort of subpersonality with its own set of charged emotions that cluster around certain areas or triggers in our lives, often a trauma. You have probably already heard many of the common complexes that have made their way into our vocabulary such as *mother complex, father complex, money complex, Oedipal complex, hero complex, Napoleon complex, Peter Pan complex, lover complex,* etc. Just hearing the title of the complexes likely brings to mind a fair amount of what they encompass. Thus, a person gripped by a money complex may irrationally fear poverty and financial need. Even though he has plenty of money, his fear drives him to hoard more and more. One might name it a *Scrooge complex* after the Charles Dickens character in *A Christmas Carol*. Those who struggle with a *hero complex*, on the other hand, may find themselves irrationally drawn toward rescuing others who may not even need their help. The more powerful a *complex*, the less aware we will be when we fall into it and the more our behavior is controlled by it. Our friends, family, and lovers, though, are painfully aware when we are in the grips of these *complexes*, even as we irrationally defend our behaviors.

A particular point of Jungian psychology is that at the core of every complex lies an *archetype*, in our drawings noted as the letter "*A*." Thus, at the heart of someone's *hero complex* lies the *archetype* of the hero. This archetype is present in hero images known throughout history and embodies all the heroic traits to which humanity has ever been exposed. We can imagine the world's most powerful hero, Hercules for example, lying at the heart of this *complex*. It is that intense energy that a person in the grips of a hero complex is tapping into. These moments can be precarious for those trapped in the complex or, on the other hand, may even result in admirable deeds.

The Archetypal Self

Within the framework of Jungian psychology, the *ego* is technically a complex where we hold our conscious self-identity. Remembering that at the core of every *complex* lies an *archetype*, within the core of the *ego complex* lies the *archetypal Self*. It can be referred to by its full name, the *archetypal Self*, or simply the *Self*. By convention we capitalize the *Self* to note its elements of totality and even sacredness, similar to how *God* & *He/His/Him* are capitalized in the Christian scripture. The *Self* is humanity's (as well as each individual's) grand organizing principle. While many have referred to the *archetypal Self* as God, it may be better to think of it as godlike with infinite, boundless possibilities that we often associate with phrases like a *higher power* or a sum of all the conscious and unconscious elements within our universe. It is *the Alpha and the Omega*, the beginning and the end, the *totality* and the *singularity* combined as one. It is hard to write about the *archetypal Self* without lapsing into mysticism and using grandiose metaphors. It is truly ineffable, and words fail to capture it.

The Primordial Fire

We added the *primordial fire* to the bottom of our map in an effort to show some of the profound archetypal forces underlying these structures. The *primordial fire* represents the initial source of psychic energy and the animating forces throughout human history and even the history of the universe. It drives survival, evolution, creativity, and such instincts as sexuality and hunger. When we are depressed, we have lost contact with the *primordial fire*. When we are manic, we may become engulfed in its flames. At times, the fire envelopes the planet, such as during the world wars or at other times of profound conflict or social upheaval. It has deep veins in the psyche, and it runs like lava beneath the crust of the earth, erupting during these intense times.

This is a collective fire that has been burning throughout the ages. Billy Joel's haunting words, "We didn't start the fire, It was always burning since the world's been turning," powerfully capture the metaphor of its ceaseless flames.

Before we dive more deeply into the ideas of *persona*, *shadow* and *ego*, here are a few suggestions that emerge from this map.

A Few Precepts to Keep in Mind....

Don't let the world define you. Blaze your own path through!

This is particularly hard for young people. There is so much to do in those early years—excel in high school and college, find the right career, find a life partner, raise children, etc. There is nothing wrong with these things, and indeed many of them are important to pursue, but sometimes these expectations are thrust upon us against our will, and they run contrary to our true nature. Looking through the lens of our map, we must be careful that the *persona* we construct retains authenticity; we must listen to our *shadow's* ferocity; we must avoid being ensnared by our *complexes* and we must tap into the inspiration of our *anima/animus*. Only by encompassing this totality, both conscious and unconscious, can we hope to discern our unique path and follow our true self.

Listen to your nighttime dreams. Keep a dream journal.

A key principle of Jungian psychology is the crucial importance of our dreams during sleep. Dreams bubble up from the collective unconscious and are informed by the *archetypal Self*. All dreams have meaning for us, telling us something we do not yet know but need to know. Write down your nighttime dreams in a journal. Reflect on them the next day and ask yourself what the various elements of the dream remind you of. Avoid the simplicity of a "dream symbol dictionary," as you will need to do the hard work yourself and not rely on someone else's interpretations. If you can, work with a Jungian analyst or other therapist who works with dreams from that perspective. Join or start a dream group where people share and reflect on dreams in a nonjudgmental and noncritical environment. Use your dreams to develop your own personalized *Map of the Soul*.

Listen to your daytime dreams. Keep a daytime journal.

Consider keeping a daytime journal as well for any thoughts, emotions, creative impulses, or in-spirations you might have. You can even write out dialogues with other parts of yourself, including *shadow* figures, *anima* figures or characters from your nighttime dreams. Notice the occasions when you undergo a reversal, and the *shadow* erupts. Ask questions and get to know these interior parts of yourself. Wonder about the present and dream about the future. Remain curious about all elements of yourself, both your interior world as well as how you interact with others. This curiosity will keep you on your path of growth.

Stay aware of your dark side (your *shadow*). Own it when it flares up and utilize its strength.

Unfortunately, ignoring our dark side is a common trap that we all fall into from time to time. We convince ourselves that we have tamed our inner darkness, only to have it reappear abruptly. When our darkness erupts, it has free rein to plunge us into various destructive paths. It is vitally important that we stay aware of our *shadow* and the hurtful prejudices, stereotypes, and superior attitudes we hold.

Stay connected to your *shadow*. Dialogue with it, listen to it, and observe how it is projected onto people and situations in your life, like a movie projected onto a screen. Acknowledge to others when your darker self has taken over and you have done things that you regret. Growth and individuation can only happen if we stay aware of our dark self and are willing to confront our less appealing qualities.

Stay connected to your body.

Avoid the trap of remaining too much in your head and disconnected from your body and the outside world. This is a trap that many Jungians and other intellectual types fall into. Looking solely at ideas, concepts, and archetypes without also looking at how they embody themselves in our physical world can prove to be a costly mistake. Listen to your body. Try to understand when it hurts, grumbles, or has a painful memory buried within it. Enjoy your body when it wants to dance, run, or play with reckless abandon.

Stay creative no matter what, and express this creativity.

Stay connected to whatever forms of creativity enliven your soul. Expressions are not only works of art like paint on a canvas, but include dance, prose, molding clay, playing music, using your voice, and countless other expressions. Creativity is a great way of tapping into the *primordial energy* in a healthy way that fuels our growth and individuation.

Know something about your personality make up, its strengths and challenges.

Stay curious about who you are and how your personality challenges and strengthens you. Seek an understanding of Carl Jung's ideas of introversion, extroversion, thinking, feeling, intuition, etc. Knowing who we are in these ways and how we engage with important people in our lives not only helps us to understand our behaviors but also helps us optimize how we engage with others.

Remember the arc of life and that young adulthood, midlife and elder years have very different callings.

It is important to consider where we are in our life's course. In our early years, we are typically building our psychic structures, our personality, our desires, our relationships, and our vocations. Hopefully, we do so with passion and a sense of calling. By midlife, we have already built these structures and we may be more occupied with a productive career, a growing family, or other challenges.

Often in midlife, there is a need for a significant course correction. We must stay alert and listen for that. By our elder years, we are on the other side of the arc of life, declining in some areas while deepening in others. We are typically exiting careers and mentoring those around us. We are often more spiritual and are nurturing our inner connection to a higher reality. While each of us needs to find our own expressions within these typical patterns, it is helpful to remember that the map serves us differently depending on the stage of our life's journey.

Remain true to yourself.

We must remain true to ourselves! But what does that really mean? Of course, it means different things to different people. We propose that it involves the vital quest of discovering what you are uniquely called to in this world. It is breaking free of the molds that others attempt to put you in as you claim your unique inheritance as a member of the human race. Regardless of how your true path unfolds, you must at all costs, listen to your gentle, whispering inner voice and honor the signs that life offers you.

The Persona

Chapter 4

An Introduction to Persona

By Murray Stein

C.G. Jung (1875-1961) was a famous Swiss psychiatrist and psychoanalyst and the founder of Analytical Psychology. After he broke with his teacher, Sigmund Freud, he created his own quite different theory and published many books and papers explaining his views. These have been gathered and published in *The Collected Works of C.G. Jung*, 18 volumes. My concept of Jung's *Map of the Soul* is an introduction to his works and a map of the ideas he put forward in his writings.

I began studying Jung's ideas when I was 24 years old and have been with it ever since. Jung's autobiography, *Memories, Dreams, Reflections*, hooked me, and I have never turned back. I find his works as exciting and inspiring as when I first discovered them in 1968. I am a practicing Jungian psycho-analyst and use his ideas every day with my clients. They have not let me down. Jung was a genius of the psyche, and his insights into how the human mind is constructed and functions are brilliant. Besides that, they are practical and intended to help people live a fuller, more creative, and more authentic life.

In traditional cultures, young people are provided with a persona role and asked to fit themselves into it. It's part of initiation into social life. A persona requires adaptation to the images offered by family and society, and it tends to stay the same throughout life. If you are a prince or a pauper, you stay in that persona. The persona places you in a social category—man or woman, aristocrat or plebe, younger brother or elder sister. Today, however, persona formation is often more individualized and therefore more challenging. People have to create a persona for themselves, one that fits their specific needs and expresses their individual personality in the present moment. What's more, as a person's needs change and his or her personality matures, the persona must also be modified accordingly. Persona management in the modern world is a much more demanding and complex business than it was in the past.

Persona is a type of mask. It hides parts of the self that you do not want to be seen by others, as well as expressing who you feel you are at the present time. Personas are created by choosing a particular lifestyle, by clothes, by hairstyle and adornments like jewelry or tattoos or piercings, by cosmetic makeup and scent, and by association with friends, a chosen profession or fan club or political party. The persona also includes behavior and plays itself out in roles that say who you are with others. But it does not say who you are when you are alone. And it is by no means all of you. The *Map of the Soul* shows a much bigger and more complex territory.

T.S. Eliot, one of the most famous English poets of the 20th century, wrote that every cat has three names: the name that everybody knows, the name that only the cat's intimate friends and family know, and the name that only the cat knows. When you see a cat sitting by itself and looking into the far distance, what is it doing? It is meditating on the name that only the cat knows, the singular, the unique, the mysterious secret name that remains hidden from everyone else.

As humans, we also have three names: the name that everybody knows, which is the public persona; the name that only your close friends and family know, which is your private persona; and the name that only you know, which refers to your deepest self. Many people know the first name, and some people know the second. Do you know your secret name, your individual, singular, unique name? This is a name that was given to you before you were named by your family and by your society. This name is the one that you should never lose or forget. Do you know it? If not, how can you discover it? This treasure may be hard to find. It is the goal of individuation to find it and claim it, and to hold on to it no matter how many times your persona may change in the course of your life.

Chapter 5

BTS, Jung and the True Self

By Murray Stein

Everything now depends on man.
(Jung, *Answer to Job, par. 675*)

I first learned about the interest that BTS had in my work from a Japanese student at the International School of Analytical Psychology in Zurich. I was pleasantly surprised to hear that my earlier book, *Jung's Map of the Soul*, was being recommended on the BTS's website. Later, when this same student informed me that the new BTS album was titled, *Map of the Soul: Persona*, I was bowled over. It inspired me to write this current book in which I could present many of the ideas I have worked with for decades. It's taken me a while to get used to the idea. I still don't know what it means but I believe it will be enormously helpful in introducing others to the profound insights that Jung gave us. I am especially happy that Jung's ideas are being popularized among younger people. The possibility that younger folks will seriously explore these themes and give attention to living more authentically, loving themselves, and thereby create a more loving world is heartening.

I have begun to listen to and study some of the earlier works of BTS. They strike me as a serious, thoughtful group of young people dedicated to the noble cause of raising consciousness, preventing mobbing, increasing self-acceptance, and fighting the plague of suicide that besets so many parts of the world today, especially among young people. They are saying that life is worth living. I support this with all my heart. And maybe the *Map of the Soul* will help support these worthy efforts.

BTS has a message. Many pop artists also carry a message, but often it's more about anger and outrage than about consciousness, identity, love, and such positive psychological developments. The ARMY fan base seems extremely dedicated and extremely respectful.

I confess to being enchanted by the way that BTS has used various books like *Demian, The Ones*

Who Walk Away from Omelas and *Into the Magic Shop* to weave complex tales full of symbolism. The band's ability to use one creative work to inspire their creative musical endeavors is fascinating. It may interest the ARMY fans to know that Dr. Jung was a man who sculpted, built a tower to which he retreated, and composed a book called *The Red Book* in which he placed astonishing hand-painted color plates and calligraphy. It is often a sign of psychological depth and flexibility to be able to be creative and even more so to create in various genres.

I don't know if attending some BTS concerts might help me understand why their message has been so influential. I suspect that BTS communicates with their fans on many levels, some of them quite nonrational. Symbols are always more than rational, and they engage our attention in ways that we can't explain. We can only reflect on the effect symbols have on us and try to understand how they are moving us.

Jung is still relevant today, perhaps more relevant than ever. The value of Jung's theories has only increased with time as people have tested them and used them in new ways. Today, Jungian psychoanalysts are located on every inhabited continent, and study groups and training programs can be found all around the world. In Korea, for instance, Professor Bou-Yong Rhi brought his Jungian training that he received in Zurich, Switzerland, to Seoul in the mid-

1960s. He has been responsible for introducing Jung's ideas to the Korean audience by translating many of his works and teaching new generations of psychiatrists at the university.

The Jungian movement continues to grow worldwide and especially rapidly in areas of the world that were not exposed to Jung's ideas before the end of the Cold War in 1990. There have been hundreds of contributors to the field of Analytical Psychology since Jung's time, and Jungian publications continue pouring out of publishing houses in many languages. I am very happy to say that Jungian psychology has a very bright future in this century and beyond.[i]

> "As one becomes a good citizen, a devoted son or daughter, a dedicated member of church, school, and state, a reliable employee, a husband or wife, a father or mother, an ethical professional, people feel confident that they can trust such a person and therefore give her or him their high esteem. Such persons speak clearly for family, community, nation or even for all of humanity, but not for themselves. If individuals who have adopted such faithful and steady personae remain unconscious of their true individuality, that individuality remains undiscovered, and they become a mere mouthpiece for the

collective attitudes that they have become identified with. While this may
serve a person's interests to a point-
because everyone after all has to adapt to
society and culture; and because a well-
constructed persona is a distinct advan-
tage for practical purposes of survival and
social success this is clearly not the goal
of individuation. It is only a staging point
for beginning the individuation process.

Understandably enough, people are tempted
to stop here, since creating a smooth and
well-functioning persona is not such an
easy thing. If identification with the personal elements that make up the persona
is an impediment to individuation on the
one hand, identification with archetypal
figures of the collective unconscious is another and perhaps even more difficult
(because more subtle) obstacle to be
overcome."[ii]

Mario Jacoby, a renowned Jungian analyst
wrote, "A strong ego relates to the outside world
through a flexible persona; identifications with a specific persona (doctor, scholar, artist, etc.) inhibits psychological development."[iii]

Chapter 6

Persona and
Your Identity

By Leonard Cruz and Steven Buser

"No man, for any considerable period, can wear
one face to himself and another to the multitude,
without finally getting bewildered as
to which may be the true."
(Nathaniel Hawthorne, *The Scarlet Letter*)

We are social beings. Our speech develops
through the reciprocal back and forth exchange with
other human beings that starts with simple cooing
noises. Facial recognition and discrimination start at
a very early age, and the persona mask we wear starts
to be crafted when we are quite young.

Face recognition ability starts from birth.[iv] Several studies have shown that by 3 months of age, infants show preferences for faces of their own race unless they are exposed to multiple people's faces of other races. This suggests that the face we present to each other and the responses that our faces evoke in one another are among the earliest dimensions of psychological development.

Our face is one of the central components that we associate with our sense of "I." We've learned that people undergoing facial transplants must be prepared for profoundly disorienting experiences when they wake from surgery to a lifetime of looking at someone else's face when they look in the mirror. Experiments with virtual reality in which a person is presented images from a point of view mounted on a mannequin that is looking at the subject can also be disorienting. Perhaps these things underscore just how much our sense of "I" is bound up with our face.

Disruptive life events that shatter one's comfortable and familiar sense of "I" often open cracks and crevices in the ego through which the light of unconscious illumination enters. The ego will try to ward off these moments since material that erupts from the unconscious is experienced by the ego as a mortal threat.

Nevertheless, breakthroughs occur. There are occasions when we are confronted with how others perceive us; however, ordinarily, the psyche is adept at self-deception. Jung's map of the soul/psyche offers us valuable insights into how this self-deception is accomplished. To a great extent, it results from the ego's rejection from conscious awareness of things it finds unacceptable. The shaping influences of early childhood, families of origin, and our culture contribute to what is rendered as unacceptable. When events occur that force us to reckon with who we "really" are instead of who we believe we are or who we wish ourselves to be, the unconscious may break through. To the extent that we go in search of unconscious contents and find ways not only to welcome them but to integrate them into our conscious life, we become more expansive, full human beings. But to the extent to which we devote ourselves to rejecting, ignoring, or numbing ourselves to the unconscious contents seeking the light of awareness, the unconscious will find other channels of expression.

> Jung said, "Until you make the unconscious conscious, it will direct your life and you will call it fate."

Too often people recognize after the fact that they unconsciously authored the tragic moments of their life. In part, this results from our inability to objectively and accurately gaze upon our own state, particularly the aspects of our state that dwell in the unconscious. The ego cannot fully gaze at itself.

Jung was acutely aware that our knowledge about consciousness is limited. We must accept that we cannot be entirely objective with regard to our own consciousness. Jung often said that psychology lacks an Archimedean point from which to view the psyche. The Archimedean point is a hypothetical point of view from which an observer can view and perceive something being studied with complete objectivity.

Modern physics has shown us that the act of observation changes the field being observed. We have learned that the observer and the observed cannot be separated.

Late in his career, Jung befriended the physicist Wolfgang Pauli. This may have contributed to Jung's appreciation for the fundamental impossibility of a completely objective, Archimedean point of reference when dealing with matters of consciousness examining itself. Just like the physicist whose observation alters the field being observed, when we turn our conscious attention to our own psyche, objectivity is lost.

We are limited by our biases. We are looking at ourselves, but not from an outside perspective. Maybe extraterrestrials could tell us more about our psyches precisely because they would have an external point of comparison.

Chapter 7

Love Yourself, Know Your Name, Speak Yourself

By Leonard Cruz and Steven Buser

The process of individuation involves communicating with and befriending the interior figures who appear. The use of active imagination (in which intentional dialogue is had with interior figures), painting and other creative arts, sand play therapy, and journaling are among the tools that help a person bring the unconscious to consciousness.

Revealing one's true self can feel incredibly dangerous. There is the risk of being rejected and ostracized. Each compromise made in service of adapting to society risks betrayal of the authentic self. The mask one wears forms with each accommodation one makes. The person who becomes overidentified with the mask he or she wears becomes distant from the authentic aspects of psyche. Lucky is the person whose persona begins to disintegrate.

If you identify strongly with a persona, after a time you will feel only what the persona allows. This gives you strength in some situations to ignore distracting emotions or attacks, but it can also prevent you from thinking in original ways. The persona restricts thinking and feeling, particularly if the mask is too tightly glued to the actor's face. They may be good actors in that specific role, but they will be out of touch when the situation changes, and the mask no longer fits well into the frame.

When the persona starts to disintegrate, the process of individuation is accelerated. The persona is a necessary psychic element, and its disintegration is likely to feel threatening. It must be remembered that hiding our true nature behind the mask—the persona—produces insidious, malignant effect. The disintegration of the persona catalyzes the process of individuation.

Remember that whatever appears in the psychic life is considered to be part of the entire self. To really love yourself, you must love ALL of your self. If you only love your ego, you miss out on the wondrous totality of who you are. This will also make you less able to love the world. The parts of your self that you fail to love or, worse yet, the parts you scorn are apt to be projected onto others. In its extreme, this can provoke hatred toward the world and others. Few people who act with brutality and malevolence perceive themselves accurately. The phrase *haters gonna hate*, a phrase popularized by Taylor Swift in her song *Shake It Off*, comes to mind.

As RM from BTS said in his address to the United Nations, "Love yourself, love the world, know your name.

> "So, let's all take one more step. We have learned to love ourselves, so now I urge you to speak yourself. I would like to ask all of you. What is your name? What excites you and makes your heartbeat?
> "Tell me your story. I want to hear your voice, and I want to hear your conviction. No matter who you are, where you're from, your skin color, gender identity: speak yourself. Find your name, find your voice by speaking yourself.
> "I'm Kim Nam Jun, RM of BTS. I'm a hip-hop idol and an artist from a small town in Korea."

I want to return to the ideas Dr. Stein put forth in his reference to T.S. Eliot's poem "The Naming of Cats." Our given name, the one by which most people know us, is deeply embedded. This is a name that we grow into, and it is mostly imposed on us. Gradually, we connect "I" with our given name. Though people can and do change their given name, this is not terribly common. While a name change disengages a person from his or her given name, such a person's sense of "I" may not change much, and there will often be others who continue to know the person by his or her given name. For example, at age 23, I met my wife, who began to call me Len, and this replaced my given name of Leonard or my nickname Lenny, except among those who only knew me before I met my wife.

There is a name that our intimates know. This is often a nickname or an endearing name like Boo or Sweetie. Even a name given by a bully is one that requires a degree of intimate connection. If a coworker were to address us by the intimate name a spouse uses, it would surprise or dismay us. This reveals that our second name is one reserved for a small cadre of individuals, the inner circle of our acquaintances. As time goes by, we also grow into our second name. The first time your girlfriend calls you "Sweetie" may stir a different effect than when she utters the same name after decades of marriage in which you've shared joys and sorrows.

Finally, there is a name that only we know. It is a reflection of our private-most self. This private name is often uttered in the regions of liminality, the in-between realms. The one who is called by that name is called by voices, ephemeral figures, and synchronistic moments that beckon to us from the deep.

When we are in touch with the ethereal realm, even inanimate objects seem to speak with a universal voice. For some people, the spirit of the depths calls out from the rocks, the trees, a book, or a song. I love books and have often sensed that a book speaks to me. My daughter is an avid rock climber, and sometimes I think a rock face whispers to her.

RM of BTS urges his fans: "Know your name." This is every person's challenge. The deepest name is the name that only we know and that sometimes even with our best effort is hard to retrieve. So much of who we are remains unconscious, and this requires lifelong, painstaking work to uncover and integrate into consciousness.

Among Orthodox Jews, great care is taken to never write or utter God's true name. YHWH is used in place of YAHWEH out of a sign of deep reverence and recognition that to use God's name would be to reduce God. Augustine of Hippo said, "If you understand, then it is not God." There is an alchemical principle that is often expressed "As above, so below." It points to the fact that the world as we know it reflects and resonates with a higher realm in which

God or the gods exist. Perhaps our third name bears a similar resemblance to the ineffable quality of YHWH.

To reach the place where our true name is found we must shake off the effects of our upbringing. We must release the fear and caution that arises from repeated hurts and wounds. We must cast off the shame associated with our mistakes. Most of all, we must recognize and free ourselves from cultural constraints. Those who accomplish this last task will be better prepared to honor our shared humanity. If you hope to live authentically you may have to go in search of your deepest, truest name.

The Shadow

Chapter 8

An Introduction to Shadow

By Murray Stein

In the physical world, the word "shadow" is defined as the absence of light behind an object that is facing a light source like the sun. In psychology, however, this word has a different meaning. If the persona is the part of your personality that is revealed to others around you, the shadow is the part of your personality that is concealed from them and even from yourself. It is a mistake, however, to think that the psychic "shadow" is nothing but the absence of the light of consciousness in a certain area of the soul. It is more than that. It is substantial, and it is active.

In psychology, shadow is a term that refers to hidden motives and attitudes. Shadow motives have an energy and a goal of their own, which are usually very different from the adapted and conformist motives of the persona. The motives are guided by unconscious attitudes, which are psychological constellations like biases and prejudices. The shadow side of the personality may be as dramatically different from the usually manifest personality as we find in the novel *Strange Case of Dr Jekyll and Mr Hyde* by Robert Louis Stevenson. The novel depicts a split personality, one of which is benign and adapted and the other criminal and psychopathic. It is a portrait of good and evil housed in a single person and alternately active in the world. The shadow is as powerful as the persona in this case.

And the shadow is complex, because it is made up not only of one but a collection of motives that serve an underlying attitude. Usually, these are motives that a person would not want others to see, so they are conveniently kept out of sight and unacknowledged. They are motives like envy and greed and cold selfishness. They work by subtle insinuation and manipulation, seeking to destroy and undermine others in order to claim superiority for oneself. Often, they are successfully hidden from sight because the persona shines its bright light in the face of others who are observing the person and receiving the treatment. They are often so well concealed and disguised that even the person who exercises them does not fully know when they are active. And sometimes they are hidden in plain sight because the persona is so powerful and distracting that people are blinded to what is happening right in front of them. We don't want to bring such motives into the light and focus on them because when they are revealed, they cause embarrassment and shame. Shame is the typical emotional reaction when a person is confronted by others with their shadow enactments or wishes, unless, that is, they are sociopaths or psychopaths, in which case they try another deceptive cover-up.

The shadow lies at the fringe of consciousness, just at or beyond the edge of consciousness and more or less out of easy sight except to the trained eye. To catch the shadow at work, we have to train ourselves to look at the fringe of our awareness and to observe our hidden thoughts and motives. It's not an easy thing to do, and we have a natural aversion to spotting the shadow in ourselves. Besides that, the fringe of consciousness trails off into the darkness of deep unconsciousness, and the further the shadow lies in that territory, the harder it is to spot. It's like trying to see a dark object against a dark background. It's nearly invisible.

Shadow-spotting is something we like to do to other people. This is called gossiping. When we point to the bad traits in other people and tell other people how awful they are, we are shadow-spotting. We might be seeing what is there, or we might be seeing our own disowned shadow that is being unconsciously projected onto another person. When we say they are "mean" or "selfish" or "greedy," we may be projecting our own similar qualities. It's very natural to project unconscious shadow traits and motives onto other people. Spotting the shadow in others is a tricky business, and we should be careful when we play that game. We may be revealing aspects of our own shadow.

A Japanese acquaintance of mine recently told me a story from her past that sharply depicts this dynamic of shadow projection. When she was a teenager, she spent a year studying in an American high school as an exchange student. As it happened and not too surprisingly, she was the only Japanese person in the school. The student body was divided into two distinct groups based on race, and there was often tension between them, as is pretty often the case in such situations. The less socially favored students felt badly treated by the more privileged ones, and there was mutual shadow projection going on between them on a regular basis. Unfortunately, the year the Japanese student was in this school was also a significant anniversary of the Japanese surprise attack on Pearl Harbor, which initiated America's entry into the Second World War, so the whole student body was made aware of the "bad Japanese" who had attacked the "innocent Americans." This created a strong bond between the two groups and among all the Americans because they could all identify with the victims of this nefarious sneak attack. And what made this bond even stronger among them was that together they could turn on the Japanese student as one of the bad aggressive people who had attacked "our country." The Japanese student felt this hostile, aggressive energy coming at her especially strongly from the young men in the less privileged group, who would call her names in the hallway and harass her on her way home after school. Here you can see how the shadow piece of the psyche—aggression and racism—was directed against the innocent Japanese girl. She became what we call a "scapegoat." This is a person who collects shadow projections from a whole group of people and is usually so badly bullied that she is forced to leave the group.

In this case, however, the scapegoat was rescued by an empathic school counselor who explained to her what was happening. The counselor's intervention was successful because she used her own experience to explain the psychology of shadow projection. She came from the same underprivileged racial group as these male students did, and she told the Japanese girl about how it was for her growing up in a rural community where she had experienced daily taunts and harassment from the other students in her school because of her racial difference. The Japanese student could then feel that in the school counselor she had a friend who understood her painful situation. As a result of this helpful insight into the psychology of shadow projection, the Japanese student decided to study psychology, and when she returned to Japan and entered the university, this was the subject she chose as her major. Today she is a school psychologist and a professor of clinical psychology in a Japanese university. The experience of receiving the projection of shadow and the importance of understanding how it works put her on a whole new and meaningful course in life. This is what we sometimes call making lemonade out of the lemons life delivers to us. Some of our most important and transformative experiences in life come from painful, shadow-filled moments like this.

Becoming aware of your personal shadow is usually not a pleasant experience, but it is the path to deeper areas of the psyche and thus essential for wholeness. Without integration of the shadow into the conscious household, something essential is lacking. Shadow integration is also the key to assuming responsibility for your actions and therefore constitutes an important contribution to the community and the world. Jung once wrote: "One does not become enlightened by imagining figures of light, but by making the darkness conscious."

The same principle applies to nations. Nations, too, have their shadows in the form of cultural biases and nationalistic selfishness. These are the dirty secrets in a nation's history, and sometimes the shadow enactments of nations are extreme, and their crippling effects pass down through the later generations. Only if they are acknowledged and made conscious can a nation recover its full identity and move forward in its cultural evolution. Nations must accept responsibility for their actions if they are to continue to grow and mature, just as individuals must. Shadow work is required on many levels. Just as Germany, for instance, has had to look at its past actions during the Nazi period of its history, and as the United States must look at its aggressions in various parts of the world on behalf of its selfish economic and political interests, so nations across the globe must delve into these shadowy areas of history and politics if their citizens are to be freed from the consequences of shadow enactments. The ancient notion of "karma" speaks to this insight. Today we speak of "transgenerational transmission of trauma" (TTT), and we can also speak of "transgenerational transmission of responsibility" (TTR), which might be called social karma.

The chapters in this little book are intended to help the reader become more aware of the many manifestations of the psyche's shadow, individually and collectively. Becoming conscious of the shadow and taking responsibility for its manifestations open the way to the next level of psychological development, which has to do with making contact with the anima and animus, the links to the center of the self. Our discussion of this level will be left for a further volume in this series on the *Map of the Soul*.

Chapter 9

The Shadow

By Murray Stein

Explorations of Shadow

Jung came up with this term "shadow"—it's original with him and is an image intended to refer to the parts of the personality of which we are not aware, that are behind our backs, so to speak. The shadow exists at the fringe of consciousness and is difficult to detect directly. You might also think of the shadow as the sum total of motivations, thoughts, feelings, and behaviors that one would not be proud of or for which one wouldn't want to accept responsibility. It is the part of the personality that normally one will not or cannot acknowledge.

The shadow is mostly shaped by a person's subjective sense of the social world around them. A person's self-esteem is highly dependent on what other people think of them. Cultures large and small, from family to large social networks, judge certain qualities to be good and admirable, like heroism or selflessness, and others like cowardice and selfishness to be bad. Even though everyone has an element of cowardice and selfishness, these qualities would be hidden from view even though they're a part of oneself. Other qualities that are not bad in them- selves morally speaking might also be placed into the shadow. For instance, some people are naturally very outgoing, or in Jungian terms extroverted, but if they live in a culture that does not look kindly upon people who are outgoing, too friendly or too demon- strative in public, they will try to tone down those qualities in their personality and repress the stronger aspects of this tendency. One tries to shut off or put away those motivations and behaviors that are not socially acceptable, that don't fit into the persona. Something that might be a natural part of a person can be discouraged and associated with feelings of shame and social disapproval. We recognize that this process of shadow-creation is a response to the social world surrounding us.

It's natural to conform to the social world around us because it's natural for us to want to be respected and esteemed. Suppose you grow up in a criminal family, where criminal behavior is valued in your family but not in the wider culture. Within the family context, your criminal behavior would be a source of respect and esteem, but you wouldn't want to show that in the general culture, or you would be punished or imprisoned. What is acceptable in one social context may not be acceptable in another, so the persona changes accordingly. People have more than one mask to draw upon for the sake of acceptance and adaptation. The shadow of a person raised in a criminal environment might actually contain features that would usually be thought of as noble and socially acceptable, but in the criminal family they would be judged as negative. On the other hand, actions that might be disapproved of in the greater society might be highly esteemed within the smaller criminal society. In a criminal family, things that are normally shunned in society might be required, respected, and produce great benefits. The makeup of the shadow thus really depends upon one is conforming to.

It is important for people to be able to perceive their shadow side. C. G. Jung stated, "We need more understanding of human nature, because the only real danger is man himself." There is a tendency we have to enact our shadow impulses and justify them without recognizing them for what they are. For example, if a country would feel itself in danger from another country, it could "defend itself" by launching a preemptive strike on the other country. Though the aggressor country might feel justified and within that national culture the first strike might appear defensible, looked at from another perspective, it would appear quite different. It might be based on projection of the shadow onto the "enemy" country. The attack on the projected shadow could bring catastrophic results and even unleash a nuclear war. This is what Jung feared. The point is that it's easy for us to justify, explain, or defend our impulsive shadow behaviors within a certain set of conventional and self-serving expectations. But in a larger sense, we can see that these sorts of actions and reactions are very dangerous and destructive.

This type of behavior happens all the time on an interpersonal level. We enact shadow impulses, and if somebody questions us about them, we defend them vigorously, because we are confident in our rationale for them. However, if we put ourselves in the other person's shoes and look at ourselves from that perspective, we may be able to see that we are overreacting due to shadow projection or using the situation as an occasion for violence or aggression or opportunism. The primary goal of becoming conscious of shadow is to step outside of oneself a bit and to look at oneself from another perspective and more objectively.

The Shadow Revealed in Psychotherapy

We can't generally see our own shadow, although we are enacting it continually in our lives. Occasionally, we can step outside our self-justified perspectives to see what we are really doing unconsciously. We can't see our own shadow, but others can see it. If you're standing in bright sunlight and facing toward the sun, you can't see that you even have a shadow, let alone what it looks like. There's nothing shadowy in front of you. But if you turn around and look the other way, or if somebody takes a picture of you from a third position, the shadow behind you will be revealed. Think of the shadow as a second personality in yourself. In one respect, you appear to yourself as conscious, light, bright, and perfectly justified in what you do. But there's another character in yourself that has other motives and agendas, and these are enacted at the same time. That is the shadow. And we are both. Both are housed in the same body.

Sometimes we can step outside of ourselves and get a glimpse of our shadow. This often happens in therapy. A person describes an event that took place recently. Say they've gotten into a dispute with their husband or their wife. They're describing it, and while the therapist is quietly listening, they might start seeing themselves through the eyes of the therapist, who is a third party, a witness. They begin overhearing themselves. They hear themselves from another person's position. The therapist may be saying nothing or may only ask a question, and suddenly a person will start reflecting. "Oh, yes. Maybe there was another agenda afoot. Maybe I was unnecessarily defensive or aggressive. Maybe I was paying him back for something he said yesterday or did last year." This can be a shocking realization. What is said to another person in psychotherapy echoes back, and so the other person becomes like a mirror. You can see things in a mirror that you can't see when you're just looking straight into the distance. In a mirror you are seeing yourself. That's why therapy can be so effective; a person is allowed just to speak, and the therapist is quietly mirroring. People start hearing themselves in another way. This can also happen when someone films you and you later watch yourself.

I had this experience years ago. I was on a program, and the discussion was being filmed. I watched the film afterward, and I saw myself on the film in a way I had never experienced myself before. I asked my wife about this, and she confirmed what I saw. It was an eye-opener. I was seeing things in the film that other people had said about me and I had brushed off. At most, I had wondered why are these things were being said about me. A lot of people don't like to see themselves on film; they don't like to see what film reveals. Why is that? It's because while watching the film, you see yourself in a more objective way. You may have an image of yourself, of the kind of person you are, what your qualities are like, and how you come across to others. Seeing yourself on film can disrupt that. It's the difference between subjective self-perception and objective self-perception. On the film, you see yourself as an object, not as the subject. When you see yourself as an object, you see flaws and other features you ordinarily are blind to or deny. It's not unlike when you look in the mirror and you see flaws on your skin and wrinkles, and you think, "Oh my goodness. I'm going to have to do something about that. I need to clean myself up." That's what therapy is really about. It is coming to a place where you can see yourself more objectively and start making some changes based on your new consciousness.

The Projection of Shadow

We know that what is unconscious to a person is projected onto external objects or people. What that means is that a person experiences those unconscious qualities, those features of their own personality, not as part of themselves but as qualities in somebody else. It is often difficult to sort out the difference between perception and projection. What are you perceiving in another person, let's say in your friend, your partner, your business associate, your boss, or your student that is really a part of them, and what are you adding to that, or layering over it something that rightfully belongs to you but that you've disowned or disavowed? It's worth asking the question even if you can't answer it definitively.

One way to catch a glimpse of your shadow is to examine the people you really dislike. Look at the disagreeable qualities that you see in them and then ask yourself, "Where are those qualities in me?" Say you're a quite successful and hardworking sort of person who has earned your way to your present status, and you really dislike people who are passive, lazy, and always looking for a handout. You may find that you have a very strong emotional reaction to those people and very little empathy for them. "Why aren't they more like me?" you ask. "I had to work hard for what I have, etc." We all know such stories in our own families and in the society at large. To catch hold of the shadow, you might ask yourself, "Where am I like that? When do I think like that?" Or perhaps, "Do I envy them?" This can put you in touch with the shadow, because the shadow is something that is very different from yourself as you know yourself consciously. It is your unlived life. When we project the shadow onto someone, we put ourselves above them and look down on them as "other." We don't feel connected to them. We judge them harshly. This is also a reflection of how we judge ourselves. We condemn our laziness and don't let ourselves take a decent vacation while condemning those who are always seemingly on vacation.

Envy is a part of almost everybody's shadow. Most people loudly deny that they're envious, because that is really a quality that very few people want or can admit to. Within the shadow you have other strong feelings that are not particularly positive or accepted as well. People can become very passionate indeed in their reactions against shadow figures.

There are certain figures in history, or certain people in our contemporary culture, that it's easy to project our shadows on, because they have qualities, objectively, that are suitable hooks, as we say, to catch the projection of shadow. Political leaders will often catch the projection of the darkest shadow. Currently in the U.S., President Donald Trump catches a lot of projections. This doesn't mean that he doesn't possess these qualities that are also projected onto him. Bear in mind that one can oppose the things that he's doing, but when people get very passionate about that and exaggerate the objectionable qualities, they fail to take into account a more complete and more complex picture. Someone like the current president represents the collective shadow of a nation that is itself trying to hide the very qualities he reveals so openly and strikingly. The more complex picture is that the nation has a shadow. This president reveals it. When we feel revulsion for him, we are facing the nation's shadow. And this is shocking. But other countries could tell us a lot about the shadow of America in the world, and it would be consistent with what we see in this president.

Let's consider racism. President Trump is often branded as a racist, which he may well be. America is notorious for hiding its heritage and continuing evidence of racism. When a figure appears who catches that projection, they are the recipient of a collective shadow projection. Many people participate in this social phenomenon but are unwilling to admit it. So, if I'm an unconscious racist, I'd love to find somebody out there who's an explicit racist, so I can label them and attack them, or criticize them. This makes it easier for me to avoid a genuine confrontation with my own racism. Projections onto a very visible figure as being racist permits me to remain unconscious to my own racism. I feel pure and project all the bad onto him. This is classic shadow projection. The object carrying the projection is a scapegoat.

I don't believe there's anybody who's not racist to some degree. If you think that you're not racist at all, you're quite unconscious. You might not be a racist in the strong sense of the word that you want to commit violence, but you have racist reactions.

Everybody does. The person who can face his or her shadow and say, "Yes, I have racist reactions, too," has a much better chance of counteracting their racism behaviorally than the person who denies it. The person who denies it enacts it unconsciously. The person who admits it and takes it into account may try to offset it consciously, or at least try to not let it interfere with his or her conscious activities and decisions.

The Shadow and Evil

At the deepest layers of the shadow dwells what Jung refers to as *absolute evil*. In a chapter in his book *Aion*, where he's talking about shadow, he implies that it is fairly easy to become aware of one's personal shadow, which is probably an exaggeration, but he goes on to say that it is a rare person who can look into the face of absolute evil. It's so horrible.

What is absolute evil? It is cold. It is brutal. It is an ego that is absolutely self-centered. It is at the core of the selfish, egotistical personality that we all have. It is that "I" in us that wants what it wants, when it wants it, at any cost, and will go to any length to get it. That is the essence of the shadow part of the personality. We don't want to see that part of ourselves. It shocks us. We don't want to admit it to ourselves, let alone to others. We shiver when we see somebody who exemplifies it, as happens in the movies sometimes. The figure who embodies absolute evil is both fascinating and frightening to us.

Conscience

Conscience is a complicated topic. On the one hand, it's our introjected values from culture and from our parents. It speaks to things like keeping ourselves clean, being nice to other people, and respecting other people's property. The 10 Commandments and other religious codes contribute contents to this level of conscience. We learn all these things, and they become a part of what we call the watchful "superego." Our conscience functions like an inner judge or policeman who tries to prevent us from exercising impulses that would violate those rules. That's a part of conscience. It consists in the rules of the family or the culture that have been taken into ourselves and made a part of ourselves as an internal moral monitor. It is on the lookout for shadow impulses and behaviors.

But that's a rather superficial level of conscience. It's something the children develop at quite an early age. Their good conduct is based on the fear of being punished for breaking the rules; out of fear they become good little boys and girls and conform to the conventions of the society they grow up in. However, there is a deeper kind of conscience, which is what we can call an innate sense of justice and fairness. It's as if we have a good angel on one shoulder and a bad angel on the other. The bad angel is the one that wants us to be 2 years old and enact our egotism and selfishness. The good angel has a sense of justice, and this one puts us on an equal footing with everybody else. It says, "Would you want other people to do that to you?" It is the root of "do unto others as you would have them do unto you." From these two voices you start getting a sense of balancing your ego interests with other people's interests. Sometimes one weighs more (self-interest), sometimes the other weighs more (altruism). There is a pendulum effect. In a sense, one is the shadow of the other.

We are constructed psychologically of opposites. If you listen to the good angel all the time, the bad angel doesn't just go away and disappear. It's there, but it works in an underhanded way, behind your back. Your selfish agendas are there, only they are well hidden. Jung said about his pastor father that in public he was all good but at home he had a very bad temper. You may be more likely to witness the shadow when good people become exhausted, stressed, or tired; they let their guard down, and a different personality appears. We saw this recently in Pope Francis, when he slapped the hand of a woman in the audience who had tried to hold onto his sleeve. He was tired and reacted with strong anger and aggression. Later he apologized, of course. He is a person who tries to live up to his office as the leader of the Roman Catholic Church, but he is also human and subject to shadow enactments.

What we have within ourselves is a kind of Dr. Jekyll and Mr. Hyde phenomenon. Mr. Hyde's a nice man by day, and Dr. Jekyll is his shadow character who works his evil by night. Our goal as Jungians is to work toward wholeness, which means finding a good enough balance between self-interest and the interests of others. Generally, we work toward balancing the opposites, not choosing one over the other. There appear to be two extremes in this regard. At one end are people whose self-absorption is so thorough that they're incapable of recognizing the other. At the other extreme are people who have such an overdeveloped conscience that they can't avoid thinking of the other most of the time. So, on the one hand, there are people with no conscience at all, whom we call psychopaths or sociopaths. They don't care about anything other than themselves. On the other hand, there are people who are so other-focused as to be almost incapable of pursuing their own interests, and this is its own sort of problem. They don't look out for themselves enough and are too self-sacrificing. In some cases, they become busybodies, and they want to help other people even when other people don't want their help. They tend to neglect themselves. What these people are not accepting in themselves is their own natural egotism and self-interest. They're repressing that, so this natural egotism becomes deep shadow. Jung once said, "It's unhealthy to be too good." In therapy we have to help them become more self-assertive and to stand up for themselves.

Balancing Persona and Shadow

As you move away from one-sidedness toward balancing the opposites, let's say between persona and shadow, eventually both sides change. The persona adjusts itself and takes up some of the shadow components. Let's say aggression, for instance, is in the shadow. When integrated, the person would become more self-assertive as a consequence, and the persona would change accordingly. This is an important aspect of psychological development. The shadow side would be less unconscious and less prone to be projected onto others. When the opposites aren't pushed apart so far, they become complements, and they supplement each other. Along with that, one doesn't have to be so ashamed of the shadow part of one's self. One can be more open about it. The shadow is part of the whole and recognized as such.

When you see people who have really done this work, they're relaxed. They're not trying too hard to be good. If you point out certain features that in a public setting might be seen as not perfect or not the best, they accept it gracefully. They aren't proud of it, but they don't try to deny it defensively. They can apologize, as we saw Pope Francis do so well.

It's been said that if you really want to know yourself, just ask the people around you; ask your spouse or your friends. What this means is that you are asking for a picture of yourself from another person's perspective. The problem with this approach is that the person you ask might have an agenda of his or her own and be trying to put you in your place and so could exaggerate your shadow aspects. Nevertheless, over time, if you listen carefully to the people around you—your co-workers, your fellow citizens, your neighbors, your friends, your family members—you will get a picture of yourself, a portrait that would include your shadow aspects. If they love you, they will say things like, "Well, I really like this about you, but when you do that, I don't like it." Listen especially to what you become defensive about, or just don't recognize, because this is unconscious to you. It is where you can grow the most.

Knowing yourself through Dreams

Another way to discover your shadow is by looking at your dreams. If you carefully study your dreams over a period of time, you'll see certain characters appearing and reappearing who are not the "I" in the dream but represent the shadow. They are generally characters of the same sex or gender that you are, but they are considerably different in ways that are unattractive to you the dreamer. Maybe they're more aggressive, more hostile, more sexual. They represent parts of your personality that you might have difficulty allowing into your every-day self-portrait and presentation.

If you assume that dream figures are parts of yourself and do not represent somebody else, you can ask yourself, "When am I like that?" and "Can I get a feeling for that part of me?" Working with the dream in this way can help you interpret it and give you insight and understanding about your shadow. For instance, I know a man who's had a lot of dreams about unruly young teenagers. At one time he had been a schoolteacher and had difficulty in his classes with some of these adolescents. Over and over again, he had dreams in which he was a teacher in a classroom full of very unruly teenagers. He is himself a very well-put-together and carefully constructed adult and now an elderly gentleman. He is not some-body you would describe as unruly. The adolescents in his dreams are unruly parts of himself that he hasn't managed to take into his conscious personality and get to know well enough. After a period of time when he had allowed himself to be a little unruly, he told me a couple of dreams in which the school-children were behaving much better. I think maybe the unruliness was coming more into his conscious personality, and he could accept it and live it in a conscious way. The unruly teenagers were changing in his dreams. He needed to become more unruly, and the dream figures then responded and changed for the better. That's a sign of integration.

Letting Your Shadow Speak

I remember a man I worked with many years ago in analysis who discovered a method for letting his shadow-self speak. It was called the two-hand method. You write something on a piece of paper with your dominant hand, and then you let your nondominant hand answer, and this goes back and forth. He was surprised by what the left hand was trying to say to him. This was a piece of himself left behind long ago in his childhood. The left hand was about 6 years old whereas in fact he was 50 years old. The 6-year-old was expressing himself as being very unhappy. The 50-year-old man asked, "Why are you unhappy? What's the matter?" The left hand, the child, said: "I want to draw and paint, and you don't let me. You don't give me any space and time to do what I want to do." He remembered that when he was about that age, his mother thought he had no talent for art, so she urged him to focus on his academic studies, and so he left the artistic part of himself behind. Now the 50-year-old went out and bought some paints and materials to create art, and the little boy started painting. That reduced the unhappiness of the little boy. His shadow became integrated through the right hand communicating with the left hand.

This is one way to let these unruly parts speak and have a voice, to find out what they want. When you give them a little space to do it, they aren't so unruly anymore and actually become an important part of your creativity.

When the child figures in our psyche are not tended to, they will often afflict us. It's quite unconscious until you catch it. We aren't trainlike mechanisms that you can wind up and let proceed. In the course of our lives, we begin in a certain direction. Are we going to be an athlete, or are we going to be a scholar, or are we going to be a BTS singer or a movie star? The effect is that other things are left behind. In fact, it's a good thing that we do that as our ego develops capacities and strength. But the problem is that what we leave behind doesn't just go away. It stays frozen in place and often festers, and it becomes like this left-handed little boy who may be unhappy, unruly, and disruptive. We may fall into bad moods, exhaustion, burnout, and various kinds of unhappiness, depression, and anxieties as a consequence of this one-sided development. Those are signals that something is amiss.

A lot of people, for instance, in their later years will pick up interests that they left behind in earlier years. That's very good for them psychologically. I know a man who started playing cello in his 60s and discovered that he had a great gift for making music. This was not allowed and not nurtured in his childhood. He had to choose another path in life, but once he got onto that musical path, he discovered a great talent in himself, and it's very meaningful to him to play the cello now. Had he not done that, he would be very unhappy in his later years and probably very envious of other people. In fact, he is one of the least envious people I know.

Envy Within the Shadow

We tend to envy people who are doing things we want to do or who have things we want but don't allow for ourselves. So we envy them. However, it's very possible that we are unconscious that we envy them. We just feel unhappy when we see or think about them. Envy is a signal of something you don't have that you would like to have but don't seem to be able to get your hands on. Sometimes you may not be, in fact, able to obtain exactly what you envy—for example becoming a star baseball player or a professional musician—but you may be able to attain a satisfactory level of involvement if you give it some time and energy. The man whose inner child wanted to be an artist did not become a Picasso, but he did enough art to satisfy his desire.

If you're unconsciously envious of people, you probably are very critical of them for having what they have and doing what they do. Unconscious envy isn't like a feeling of, "Oh, I wish I had that." It's more like a hatred for the one who has what you envy but can't let yourself admit it. With conscious envy we covet what the other has; whereas with unconscious envy, is it more likely that we may want to destroy or disparage what the other person has. Coveting means you feel you want it. Covet your neighbor's wife: "I wish I had a beautiful wife like that." That's David's story with Bathsheba. And then he gets what he wants, but he commits a terrible act, namely murder of her husband, to get her. He pays dearly for that and confesses his guilt for the rest of his life. But unconscious envy is that you want to destroy the other person who possesses it. For instance, people who unconsciously envy wealthy people, if you ask them, "What's going on? Why are you so critical of that person?," they'll never say, "I wish I had what they have." They'll say, "Well, I don't want to be rich myself, but look at what they're doing with their money, look at how badly they treat other people. They should be taxed. We should confiscate their money. They should be punished." Unconscious envy is destructive. We see how people can be mobbed, for example, on Facebook and other social media platforms. A lot of that is envy driven, and it's extremely destructive.

Mirroring and the Narcissist

If you're working with a patient who is quite narcissistic or is very sensitive to criticism for whatever reason, maybe from past traumas, you have to be very careful about approaching the shadow. You must practice what M.-L. von Franz called "bush politics" with the shadow. In other words, if you approach the shadow, you must behave as if you are in the jungle approaching a foreign tribe. The tribe members don't know who you are. They can't trust you. When they see you, you must wave white flags to let them know you aren't going to hurt them. You have to bring them presents. You have to tell them how wonderful they are. Then they'll let their guard down enough to let you in closer.

With a lot of patients, you have to practice what we call positive mirroring and empathy before you can ever start approaching anything to do with the shadow. They will bring shadow issues up indirectly, and you can only listen and mirror your support. In time, you can ask a few questions. But if you start looking at them from another perspective other than their own, and they are very sensitive to criticism and narcissistically vulnerable, you'll make yourself into an enemy. Then they'll see you as one of those people who don't like them and who want to destroy them.

The reason some narcissists don't pay attention to anybody else is that they can't take criticism at all. They just seal themselves off from any outside perspective because they can't bear the slightest hint of another perspective. So, when working with shadow material in analysis, the analyst generally will be very careful and alert for instances where the shadow is appearing and speaking for itself, as in a dream. Just by listening to patients' stories and helping them to overhear themselves a bit will over time improve their ability to reflect on themselves. The problem with narcissism is there's no self-reflection. It's usually empty of self-reflection. The mirror the narcissist looks into shows only positive and ideal features. It does not tell the truth. When it does, there is an outburst of narcissistic rage, as we see in the story of Snow White, for instance. The narcissist is looking in a mirror but seeing only the persona.

The analyst, on the other hand, sees the positive value of shadow. If you can frame shadow in a positive way, the narcissist can hear it and they can do something with it. For example, if a narcissist has a hugely negative reaction to somebody and comes and reports that to you, that somebody insulted him or her, or did something hurtful and the narcissist had a huge reaction against that, you can cast that reaction in a way that makes them feel OK about it but helps them to reflect on it at the same time. You can say, "You certainly took care of yourself in that situation. You needed to defend yourself!" and that will bring up a moment of reflection, and maybe they'll begin to consider, "Well, I probably didn't need to do it that much."

People who aren't aware of their shadow give you a kind of two-dimensional experience. They may be very fascinating or attractive at first, but you very quickly get tired of it because it just repeats itself and it doesn't go anywhere. If people are able to see their multidimensionality and not hide what are called typically shadow aspects, they'll be able to laugh at themselves. They have a better sense of humor, they'll have more depth, and they're less predictable. So, you can have a much more interesting conversation with such people than you can with those who are really locked up in the persona and is locking out any shadow aspects. They make you uncomfortable because you sense they're hiding an essential part of themselves, their emotional reality.

The Collective Shadow

The collective shadow is the sum of many personal shadows magnetized in a certain direction. Think of metal filings: You can put the metal filings on a piece of paper, and then you move a magnet underneath the paper, and this makes the filings move in a direction in line with the magnet. In the collective unconscious, there is an archetypal shadow. It's innate, inherent, always was, and always will be. The archetypal shadow collects the personal shadows of the group members and moves them in the direction of the magnet. The magnet is the group leader, the *Führer*, as the Germans call him.

In modern times, the classic example of this phenomenon is what happened in Germany in the 1930s. Within a few years, people were drawn into a political movement that previously had existed only latently but had not been directed forcefully in a particular direction. The collective shadow was "constellated," as we say. The leaders collected the resentment and envy that was resident in the national psyche, and using the long-standing native anti-Semitism that had been residual in German and European culture for centuries, they found a powerful magnet that could move the individuals like filings on the surface of a piece of paper. The leaders, especially Adolf Hitler, discovered that by using anti-Semitism, they could mobilize people's emotions and point them in a certain direction of action, albeit with catastrophic consequences.

Certain political elements in the United States have done the same thing with racism. There are residual strains of racism that can stir emotions like fear and hatred and be directed in certain directions for political gain. You can see that working in the country today. The unconscious racism, which is a part of the collective shadow in the country, can be stimulated and activated and used politically. People very naively thinking they're not racist will vote for a racist, because they have racist elements un-consciously. In the collective, the shadow activity becomes very dynamic, because many people are participating in it and giving it energy, consciously or unconsciously.

At the deepest level, shadow is evil. It's the will to destroy. In the Bible, the first incidence of serious shadow activity is murder, when Cain kills his brother, Abel. Cain gets very angry because Abel's offering is preferred by God. His offering is accepted, while Cain's is not. Cain gets very angry at his brother. God comes to him and says, "Cain, you're very angry. Be careful. Sin is lying at the flap of your tent." He adds: "Evil is lying at the door. But you can manage it." But when Cain goes out of his tent, the shadow gets him, and he takes his brother into the fields and murders him. That thing that's lying at the flap of the tent is archetypal evil. It's at the core of the shadow—in the collective, and in the individual—and it collects emotions like resentment and envy, pride and lust and all the other destructive emotions around it. If we fall into its grip, we become it, even if only momentarily. We become possessed, and this can happen to individuals and to nations. Once it becomes tribal, it's very hard for the individual to resist its intoxicating effect. Evil lurks in the collective unconscious, and you can easily succumb to it.

You often succumb to it before you know it. Your emotions take you there. I'm talking about the way in which people are like the metal filings and can be magnetized, galvanized into a certain direction. It's emotional. It's mob psychology. Emotion captures people and takes them where it wills. So, we see these rallies where people are shouting and screaming, and they're largely unconscious of what they are participating in. When you take individuals aside and quietly ask them what they are shouting about and enthusiastically supporting, they often don't know.

Fortunately, good can also mobilize in a similar way. We can become possessed by ideals and noble values. We don't just have bad archetypes; we also have good ones. We have the savior, we have very light and noble Ideas. Justice is one. There are gods and goddesses of justice, weighing the scales. Justice and compassion. And we have symbols of justice like the Statue of Liberty, which are capable of galvanizing us with our noble thoughts and motives, and people will sacrifice themselves for that. People can be magnetized to make great and noble sacrifices for the good, just as unconsciously as people can be galvanized unconsciously to rape and murder.

In the individual psyche, certain memories and experiences cluster around archetypal cores and form complexes. The same thing happens at the level of the collective psyche. You have these magnets at the bottom of the collective unconscious, and material gathers around the magnets, and individuals are drawn into or captured by them. Then they can be manipulated. The force that draws and holds the filings together is emotion. For instance, if you have strong feelings of a need for revenge, as the Germans had after the First World War, and you locate the enemy—in this case the Jewish people—the emotions gathered around this need for revenge get drawn into this vortex. People at the collective level begin to think, "We're going to eliminate this cancer from society." This feels like a good and noble thing to do for the collective. The emotion behind this is intense, and some people will feel very noble about carrying out violent and destructive actions even to the point of self-sacrifice. Religious zealots do the same thing. In the name of the good, they fall in the hands of the evil that waits at the flap of the tent.

So at times like this, we might ask: "Where does this strong emotion in me come from?" And if you can do that, then we can make a conscious choice about what political or collective movements to give our energy to. You can participate in a great collective movement but not do so as a part of the mob. Instead, you can do it for conscious reasons. A person might think, "I'll do it because I've thought it through, and I can agree with the principles and I can agree with the direction." We hope the courts and the justice system will operate that way, from a principled position and not from an emotional political position.

BTS and Celebrity

I can tell you that what impressed me most about BTS was a talk that RM (a member of BTS) gave before the United Nations. This was a year or two ago. In the talk, he spoke about himself. He said, "As a group, and as individuals, we've achieved great celebrity and fame. But I know I'm not that person who is the celebrity. I come from a small village, quite a ways from Seoul, the capital, and I remember my roots. I remember who I am. I remember where I came from." That reassured me that the leader of this group has maintained a sense of himself, apart from his hugely celebrated persona, and not fallen victim to the seductions of fame. He is a very gifted dancer, singer, rapper, and performer. I hope that all the members of the group stay similarly close to themselves. If they do, it might prevent them from being used by powerful forces for ulterior motives, such as political motives, or financial motives, or some other less noble purposes. Their message is a good one, it's useful, and it's critically important for the young fans who follow them. If the fans really get the message, and not simply fall into the glamour of it all, they can benefit from BTS. I hope that BTS will manage to continue to be aligned in a direction of wholesome awareness, consciousness, development, and balance. This is what they're putting forward in their message of psychological maturity and development, which we call individuation.

Celebrity brings a level of responsibility to BTS that I doubt they ever anticipated when they started singing and dancing as young boys. My impression is that some of them at least are aware of that, and they want to do the right thing. They show themselves as serious and demonstrate to their fans the value of striving for psychological maturity.

BTS, of course, comes out of South Korea, which is rooted in a very traditional Confucian and Buddhist culture. It tends to be a very conservative culture. These BTS performers, however, don't look very conservative, with the color of their hair and their body movements. I think they're trying to break out of a traditional culture and show another way, something more international. In traditional cultures, people tend to get trapped in age-old habits of behavior and attitude, and individuals are not much valued. I think BTS is helping in the modernizing of Korean culture, in the sense that individuals will be more valued for their various gifts and qualities. BTS encourages people to develop themselves more as individuals than just as members of a society or as part of a collective.

What has been very helpful for me, personally, has been how the awareness of shadow makes one humble. It makes you human. My best helpers, in this regard, have been very dear friends, spouses, and colleagues who can show me my failings and my shadow side. It is human nature to be something of a know-it-all who thinks, "I know better and I've got the answers." These people show me the mistakes I make in a humorous way, with laughter, and that lightens the load considerably. If it's not a dire and dreadful accusation, but a story told with a sense of humor, you can laugh at yourself and start watching yourself in a friendlier way than you might when you feel too accused and too guilty about shadow enactments.

The Ego

Chapter 10

An Introduction to Ego

By Murray Stein

A description of the psyche can begin at any number of points. In previous books we have taken a survey of the persona (*Map of the Soul: Persona*) and the shadow (*Map of the Soul: Shadow*), which consist in our social identities and our hidden motivations. If we think of the psyche as a house, the persona is the front facade, which faces the street and projects what real estate agents call "curb appeal." It is our self-presentation to the collective world around us. The shadow is a character who lives in the basement, a part of the personality that is hidden from the world outside and even from the inhabitants who live on the floors of the house aboveground.

The present book is about the ego (*Map of the Soul: Ego*). The ego is the character who is called "I" and occupies the ground and first floors of the house. "I" thinks it is in control of the house and plays the role of "the boss." It is the focal figure, the protagonist in the story, and feels entitled to the claim of ownership of the house. All the other characters who live in house with the ego are there because they are connected or related to the ego in one way or another. They make up what we call the contents of consciousness, and they are there in full view and behave as though they are under the ego's control, even if often they are not as controlled as they seem. They are the close relatives and are more or less well known, unlike the shadow who lives in the basement. The ego is somewhat aware of the persona but less aware of the shadow. Both are on the fringes of consciousness, and the ego does not pay much attention to them unless there are problems.

I will speak of the ego as "I" or "it" in order to avoid attribution of gender. With respect to the ego, there is essentially no difference between men and women, as we shall see. As far as this agency is concerned, the genders are equal. The owner of the house may be "she" or "he," and therefore in order to avoid any bias one way or the other I will speak of ego without reference to gender.

The ego is also what we call our "will." The fuel of the psyche is "energy" (sometimes called "libido" in Jungian circles but without reference to sexuality), and the ego has a certain amount of free energy at its disposal. To an extent, it can choose what it wants to do with the house—let's say the color of the walls, the pictures hanging on them and commemorating the ancestors, and the other objects that have been collected and remembered over time. The ego has some power to change these aspects of the house, if it wills to do so, and to make decisions that can introduce alterations large and small. It can change its surroundings and relationships to a large extent but not totally. Often the ego believes it has more freedom to make decisions than it actually possesses. This is a common illusion and probably necessary for the sake of self-confidence and self-esteem.

The ego does have some specific qualities in the individual, a type of character surrounding the neutral core. This character is sometimes described in typological terms: a tendency toward introversion or extroversion, toward thinking or feeling, toward sensation or intuition. The character style of the ego can be discovered by taking type inventory tests like the Myers-Briggs Type Inventory (MBTI) or Gifts Compass (GC). Both are available online and can help people take a look at their ego typology in an objective fashion.

To discover the core of the ego, however, it is necessary to introspect deeply, to look in the mirror, not at the dressed-up persona but at the naked person. If you ask yourself, for instance, "What is it in me that thinks this thought or feels this feeling?" and take a careful look at that part of yourself, you will begin to get a sense of the essential ego. It is a still small center of consciousness.

The ego tends to become intimately identified with its surroundings and with certain values and words, like a name. Here is an exercise: Try to separate your "I" from your given name (Jane or John) and your family name (Smith or Jones), then from your neighborhood and city and country, from memories good and bad. As you peel away these identities, you will be left with the essence of what the ego is: pure self-consciousness. It's a central point of reflexive consciousness. The ego is the center of consciousness.

While the ego is identified with many things such as given and family names, nationality, gender, race, etc., it is identified to an even larger extent with the physical body. Actually, the ego is an intimate aspect of the body it occupies. It is the body's center of consciousness, and it makes it possible for that body to become aware of itself as separate and independent and to take care of itself. This makes the body aware of its individuality and uniqueness. The ego is the "I" of the body, and every human body has one.

A client recently said something to me that puzzled me at first. She had recently suffered from a minor illness and told me: "My body knew I was sick before I did." She was referring to some physical symptoms that had gone unnoticed but could have given her ego a clue of the coming illness. She also had some dreams that in retrospect indicated the coming illness. Here she was using the word "I" in two different senses: first, as a part of the body ("my body knew I was sick") as though "I" and the body are one; second, as separate from the body (before "I" did) as though "I" and the body are two. The first refers to the body as "I," and the second refers to the ego as "I." The two "I's" are different but also the same. This is a paradox of the human psyche. The ego can separate itself from the body, and then it becomes a virtual reality in its own right.

We spontaneously make this distinction/confusion all the time without noticing it. And we can do this because the ego is self-conscious, that is, it is conscious of itself as a distinct psychic entity and separate from the body or anything other in the environment. The philosopher René Descartes made the famous statement as he was developing his theory of knowledge, "I think therefore I am." Here he is separating his "I" from the rest of his body and the world around him and identifying it with his cognitive function. But the "I" can also be separated from thinking, as he implicitly does when he says, "I think." What is the "I" that is doing the thinking? It is not the thought or the function of thinking. It is separate even from such inner activities as thinking and feeling.

Many philosophies question the reality of the ego. Does the ego really exist, or is it nothing more than a product of reflection, like an image in a mirror. An object seen in a mirror is not real, it is only virtual. It is a kind of illusion. But then, we may ask, what about the mirror? Is the mirror real? Not the image in the mirror (our "identity"), but the mirror itself? Something in us is doing the mirroring.

In truth, the ego is the mirror and not the contents in the mirror. The contents in the mirror are the contents of consciousness and separate from the ego just as the images in a mirror are separate from the mirror. The mirror (the "I") has psychic reality, similar to the other aspects of the psyche such as shadow and persona and the contents of the personal and collective unconscious. Now, if we step back for a moment and reflect on the mirror itself, we ask a still deeper question: What is it that is now doing the reflecting? It is a reflection on reflection itself, one mirror looking at another mirror. We are in a hall of mirrors. And this is still the ego. It is the ego reflecting on itself until it becomes so purified that no contents remain, only a pure reflective surface.

The ego is the center of whatever conscious-ness we might have or be able to develop. If there is consciousness of any kind, there must be an ego to register it. This was Jung's argument in contrast to the philosophies that deny the ego's reality. As long as there is consciousness, there is also this psychic factor called the ego. No matter what is being experienced, even "the void" itself as Zen Buddhism speaks of it, the ego is there as the recorder of it, as the "I" that is having the experience. In a sense, the "I" and the experience are one (as phenomenology has it), and in a sense they are not but are rather more like a mirror and the images reflected in it. They are hard to separate, but in truth they are two aspects of an experience.

Sometimes the ego is front and center, as when we say: "I want," "I will," "I can." But sometimes it is in the background as a witness to what is happening. If we feel a strong emotion, we may become totally identified with it, as when we say, "I am sad" or "I am afraid." Or we remain apart as when we say: "I am feeling sadness" or "I am filled with anxiety." The one statement shows the ego as the central character in the story; the other shows the ego as witness to an event. A strong ego can do both. It can assert, "I will!" and take action, and it can contain thoughts, feelings, and fantasies without acting on them or identifying totally with them. When we speak of a strong ego, we mean that it can act and it can contain. (As an aside, the ego that is represented in the musical album *Map of the Soul: 7* by BTS is a strong ego: able to suffer and able to act.)

The ego has to deal with both inner and outer realities that lie beyond its control. When we speak of inner realities, we are talking about powerful emotions, memories positive and negative (even traumatic), fascinating and horrifying ideas, alluring and grotesque fantasies, pulsating impulses and so forth. Sometimes we speak of "complexes," which are autonomous energies of the inner world that can have a huge impact on how the ego feels and behaves. Or we reference "instincts," which are powerful drives urging us to act immediately in order to satisfy their urgent cravings and desires. The ego has to manage these inner forces and try to balance their demands with other pressures that come from the world without. The instinct may say: "Eat! Now!" But the ego may have to say: "Wait! It's not time to eat right now." The ego is sometimes successful in moderating the demands of the inner world, and sometimes it is not and acts out. The same holds for demands made by the outer world. The ego must respond to them and weigh them against other considerations like values, integrity, ambition, and so forth.

The ego is responsible for our sense of reality inner and outer, and as such, it confronts the demands of fantasy and drive within and social and political messages from without. Time is a crucial factor in the reality of the material world around us. The ego has to take note of this factor and balance the demands of desire and reality. Sometimes this creates painful frustrations and conflicts. It is a feature of a strong ego that it can bear a lot of frustration and can hold the tension of opposites.

Jung takes note of five instincts: hunger, sexual desire, the urges to be active and to reflect, and creativity. The first two are familiar as instinctual forces in human nature, a part of physical existence and survival, and they cause a lot of problems if they are not well managed by the ego. The need to be physically active and in motion is partially physically based and partially psychological. The urge to be active is very strong and can run out of control. It becomes an addiction when it can no longer be modulated by the ego. Sometimes the muscles scream for action, and only a strong ego can say: "It's midnight. This is not the time for running in the park." The other two—reflection and creativity—are not generally thought of as instincts because they are not as directly based in physiological processes, but it is useful to think of them in this way because they also make powerful and sometimes almost irresistible demands on the ego. The instinct for reflection can drive people to excess and exhaustion. It is the source of high culture on the one hand, but it can also become a destructive tyrant on the other. And people with a strong instinct for creativity will testify that this "daimon" can take control of the ego and drive it to extremes that are not healthy. The ego can become possessed by the energies of the instincts and thus lose control of the household it is supposed to be managing.

The ego needs to be strong in order to manage the forces that make their claims. Like a muscle, it gains strength by pushing back against resistances. I learned about this type of muscle building by watching a college classmate doing isometric exercises. He was a powerfully built athlete and would stand in the doorway to his room pushing on both sides with his arms for minutes at a time. He was building his arm muscles by pushing as hard as he could against immovable objects. For some people, studying a subject like mathematics is like doing isometric exercises and has the same effect on their ego strength: It is a totally impossible task, but by staying with the frustrations and holding the tension, they are building their capacity for dealing with psychological frustrations and conflicts that will inevitably arise in life. Jung once said that the really important problems in life cannot be solved, they can only be outgrown. The ego may not only survive the struggles but grow in strength from them. Dealing with frustration is a path to ego-building.

At the extreme, one thinks of the figure of Job in the Bible. God allows Satan to arrange things so he will lose everything he has, only not his life. He suffers the maximum degree of loss—children, wealth, reputation—and he is left to his own devices without assistance from his wife or so-called friends. But he has the fortitude to hold out despite all the frustration dealt him by his friends and the devastation delivered by Satan, and finally in a tremendous vision, he gains knowledge of the Divine and manages to outlive his personal catastrophe.

Indeed, in the end he is blessed with more than he had at the beginning of the story.

Many folk tales and fairy tales tell a similar story. The character who can endure the tests and trials in the end wins the prize. This is the outcome not especially for the clever but for the resilient. Resilience is a quality in the ego much to be prized. It should be a primary goal of the ego's education and development. (The final song of BTS's album *Map of the Soul: 7*, titled "ON," expresses and celebrates this virtue impressively.)

Chapter 11

The Ego

By Murray Stein

When we think about the ego, or we are in the ego, it seems as if it's the center of the world. It seems as if it's the most important part of the psyche because it's the position or seat that we occupy. Moreover, we delineate the world by our ego; that is, we put ourselves in the center of the world. So, if we were to make a map of the psyche, based on the ego's position and perception, we'd put the ego right in the middle, the most important figure of the entire map.

But we know that the ego is actually something of a pimple on the body of the psyche. It's much smaller than the psyche as a whole. If you think of the entirety of the unconscious, it is immensely larger than the ego. So when you want to map the psyche, the ego has to be put in perspective. We could compare the ego to the sun. Planets revolve around it. The sun is the center of our solar system, but the sun itself is a part of a galaxy of millions of stars. And so, if you look at the sun in the perspective of the whole galaxy, you see that it is small and, indeed, almost insignificant when taken as a part of a whole. So that's a way of thinking about the ego. It is important but it also takes itself too seriously.

Ego versus Persona

The persona is the mask that the ego puts on itself in order to adapt to the world. In a sense, the persona is a function of the ego, and it serves the ego's purposes to adapt itself to the social and cultural situation. But in the end, ego and persona are closely related. It is possible for the ego to identify so thoroughly with the persona that the ego doesn't realize there's even a difference between itself and the persona. In fact, most people are not aware of their persona because it's so closely glued to the ego that it's the primary perception of who one is. You dress yourself up and take care of your appearance so as to be presentable to the group or the culture of which you want to be a part. The ego is a part of that and is in the world. The ego is interested in the world, and it needs to adapt to the world. The ego and the persona differ, but these differences are more functional than structural. For instance, suppose you are the head of a clinic, or you are a doctor or a teacher; then, in those roles you assume a particular persona that's fitting to that position. When you arrive home and you are with your family, you are no longer in that role, but that is not to say you're a different person. From time to time, you might catch a glimpse of the difference by noticing how you are with the people in your professional life and how you are with the people at home. That would give you a clue as to what persona you're wearing in those situations. Each of those situations would still be encompassed by ego. The ego is functioning, and it is using the persona to adapt to situations. Now, at home, you're also in a persona of sorts. If you're a father of children: You're playing that role. It is a role you've identified with, and you take it seriously, you feel it's a really important part of your life. But still, you do play a role for the child. You're an authority figure. You have to set boundaries. Sometimes you have to structure the physical and emotional. So, you have to take responsibility for that, and when you do that, you're doing it as a "father figure." That is a persona.

Looking Inward

As the ego comes to know the unconscious, the result is not necessarily a pleasurable sense of well-being, but rather a more conscious sense of self. Because of our sensory apparatus, we're looking out at the world around us most of the time and dealing with it and adapting to it and functioning in it. When the ego turns inward instead of facing outward and looks at the unconscious, it comes upon features of personality that might be contradictory to the persona or to its sense of self.

In Jungian psychology, we talk about confronting the Shadow or becoming conscious of the Shadow. This is usually an uncomfortable realization or experience because the Shadow is made up of those parts of ourselves that we would like to look away from, perhaps even hide from ourselves or other people to avoid shame or embarrassment. When you descend into the basement of the psyche, so to speak, into the unconscious, you come across these features.

Freud did his self-analysis in the 1890s after his father died. He engaged in enough analysis of his own dreams, and out of that experience he wrote *The Interpretation of Dreams*, probably Freud's best book. What he discovered when he looked at his dreams in free association with them were features of himself that he found quite distasteful. He recognized that he was competitive, he was envious, that he felt guilty about his misdeeds in certain cases.

In other words, he was becoming conscious of himself.

This awareness of those parts of ourselves that we usually hide from, repress, or suppress are one of the first things we discover when we start looking at the unconscious. When you go deeper into the unconscious, you might discover your animal nature as an extension of the Shadow to some extent. This, too, is a part of your physical nature. People dream about animals a lot, and if you look at the animals and what they symbolize, we can see features of the personality that might be uncomfortable or distasteful to the person, but they give us important information about our nature.

It's much better to be aware of this than to be unconscious of it because if you're aware of it, you have a chance to offset its effects a bit, to protect other people from the effects of your Shadow or your animal behavioral instincts.

It's a little bit like becoming conscious of coronavirus in your environment. It's not a pleasant thing to think about, but it's better to be aware that it's out there than to be unaware. If you are aware, then you can protect yourself from it and protect other people. If you discover you've been infected with the virus, you wear a mask so you don't spread it to other people.

Looking Upward

But there are also parts of the psyche that are much more pleasant to contemplate, including various Archetypal images, spiritual aspects of our unconscious selves. As we fill out the knowledge of the self as we experience it in our dreams, imagination, and so on, we realize there is a balance between the positive and the negative. Jung spoke about the self as a union of the opposites. It's made up of opposite features, qualities, tendencies, and these balance each other out so that you get a mandala-like picture, a round, 360-degree picture of the self, insofar as you're able. And the various features balance themselves out against their opposites, in that circle or mandala.

The ego also has an impulse that draws it toward more noble or inspiring or expansive aspects. We define the ego as the center of consciousness, but it's more than that. It's also a container that has active features. One of those active features is curiosity and an interest to learn and to expand the consciousness that surrounds it. So, unless the ego is heavily defended against painful topics or not wanting to look into the darkness of the unconscious or explore the world, as long as the defenses don't get in the way, the ego is interested to know more. It's like an epistemological instinct. We want to know.

That certainly was strong in Jung's makeup, perhaps his strongest instinct: He wanted *to know*, to understand. He was very curious about himself and the world around him.

Ego's Resistance and Stages of Transformation

The ego resists change and experiences transformation as a sort of death. Transformation is a kind of death and rebirth process, so demise isn't the correct word. It's a fear of dying. An analyst, David Rosen, who wrote on suicide, called it *egocide*. We undergo the experience of transformation several times in our lives. There are big periods of transformation and there are much smaller ones, but a big one is transformation from childhood to adulthood, and that period is called adolescence. During adolescence, we're going through a transformation from being a child to being an adult, but there's a lot going on physically, physiologically, and psychologically in our being. An adolescent takes a new form, develops a new sense of identity, and begins to function in the world in quite a different way.

Another period of transformation is midlife, when we move from the first half of life into the second half of life, classically around the ages between the late 30s and the late 40s. Then there's another one at the end of life in old age. This is when one retires or begins to withdraw from one's activities and develop other interests, maybe spiritual interests or reflections that are not so much engaged in an active way in the world.

But each of these transitions is a transformation process that includes a death and rebirth, a death to what has been and a birth to new possibilities, and that includes a new sense of identity. So you could think of metaphors like the caterpillar turning into a butterfly. There's an in-between stage in the cocoon, where the caterpillar melts down and dies to what it was, and a new form appears with wings, and then it comes out of the shell as a butterfly. This is also like a snake shedding its skin, and when it outgrows that skin, once again it sheds. Having grown a new skin, it goes on in its life.

These periods of transformation typically include death anxiety. Adolescents have a lot of it. It sets in yet again at midlife. People typically experience death around them. Death anxiety is very much a part of that midlife crisis. And again, at old age when death is becoming more and more of a present reality. Resistance to change can be strong, and the psyche often forces change upon a person; people seldom go into it voluntarily. You see that especially going into old age with people going to great lengths and spending a lot of energy and money to maintain an identity that probably is no longer really appropriate for them in their stage of life. With each transformation we become a new kind of person with a new or different identity. If people can relax and accept that change may not be necessarily bad, if they can go with the flow and move through it in a graceful way, they may realize these transformations as simply a part of life.

Basic Trust and the Early Years

What helps to organize and solidify the container of the ego consciousness? The most important thing in the earliest years of childhood is a reliable environment; that is, a reliable physical, emotional, and interpersonal environment. The young person is basically helpless in the world at first and instinctively relies on caregivers to provide the necessary containment, nurturance, protections, protective surroundings. If that's not there, a serious compromise in ego development can take place. Anxieties can haunt a person for the rest of their lives because their initial environment was not reliable or was not suitable, was not tuned into the needs that they had as an infant.

What contributes to the formation of a strong ego in the long run is a consistent and reliable environment in the early years. It doesn't have to be perfect, but it has to be *good enough*, as Donald Winnicott said, to allow the ego to feel some confidence in the basis of life that the child will be held and cared for. And if that base confidence, that basic trust, as Erik Erikson described it is not there, the kinds of anxieties that emerge can have profound effects.

The lack of basic trust can remain a part of the ego and really hinder the ego from developing a sense of confidence in itself and in life during the later years.

Early Trauma

Upon the basic structure of the early years, other aspects of the personality form like accretions. If the early years are filled with trauma and neglect, these early scars may remain evident in the later years. However, the psyche has tremendous resources for self-healing. This has been demonstrated in therapy with children. For example, consider the work of Eva Pattis Zoja with children from very troubled or war-torn areas of the world who had suffered severe trauma or who had suffered as migrants or who were abandoned in orphanages. She discovered that sandplay sessions over a period of 10 weeks with an adult observer had tremendous reconstructive effects on the child's attitude toward himself or herself, toward others, and that the child's behavior in school showed improvement. She mentions the immense resources for healing the psyche has within itself if the opportunity is provided for it to emerge and to heal itself.

A lot depends on what happens after people are traumatized. Are they in a situation where they can have guided therapy that will allow them to work that through and let the psyche use its resources for healing? Or does the trauma become embedded in the psyche in such a way that it continues to interfere with the good, normal ego development in the future. I don't underestimate how much the psyche can heal itself, but it needs an opportunity to do that, and that's why we're around as therapists.

The environment the ego relies upon for its proper development should be attuned to the needs of the infant. What happens is if it's not well attuned, or if it's totally unattuned, is that the infant can survive physically and grow and look more or less intact and functional, but there is such an underlying anxiety about safety and security that it develops excessively active and strong defenses against any possible dangers that the child may face. A strong ego is not fragile; it can face dangers, get bounced around, suffer failures and losses, and still it recovers. But a fragile ego cannot take very much before it breaks. If there isn't a good beginning with a solid, stable, reliable environment, this kind of fragility develops. To protect themselves, these people then build up enormous defenses so that if they ever come close to being wounded or attacked, or engage in situations where there is some possibility of suffering, they practically become like wild animals. It's what we observe with borderline personality disorder: huge amounts of rage and anger, attacking others before they themselves can come under attack. It is a sort of paranoid, schizoid defense because of this feeling that they are in danger, so they exaggerate the danger. That exaggeration comes from their early experience.

I'm thinking of a person I worked with for a number of years who was put into an orphanage when she was born and brought back home by her parents when she was about 6 to 9 months old. She never did attach well to her parents after that. The orphanage provided only the most basic care, it wasn't regulated, and there wasn't really enough food for the children, so it was a struggle to get through life. This woman is strong physically, but she has this hair-trigger sensitivity to being insulted or attacked or demeaned, so that she will size you up immediately, and either you're a friend or a foe. You're either on her side or you're on the enemy's side. That all stems from this early sense of insecurity that was built into her system, and the defenses are there to protect her. She's a lovely person if she's not threatened. But if she is, becomes very violent.

Exposure to severe, repeated trauma, and maybe even intentional cruelty can have a very lasting impact, and often this depends on the age and the kind of abuse. One of the problems that can develop is an enormous sense of guilt and low self-esteem because people feel responsible for the bad things that happened to them. They come to believe that they were bad and that it was their fault that a parent abused them (whether physically, sexually, verbally, or emotionally). They take in those messages of "You're bad," "It's your fault," or "If you say anything, you'll be punished," so the trauma becomes a secret, and the guilt builds. In order to offset that, they might develop defense mechanisms that tell them that they're OK. For instance, they look for affirmation from other people. This is the problem with those with narcissistic personality disorder. They can't affirm themselves, so they have to get it from the outside. They don't have the inner resources to say, "I'm OK. I'm fine. I've done a few things bad or wrong, but I can forgive myself and work it through." Instead of that, they have to get the affirmation from outside, so they perform to get the gleam in the eye of the others and to get affirmation from other people around them. It becomes a mirror in them. Everyone is a mirror for them—do they like me, admire me—but deep underneath this, there is a deep anxiety. If the acclamation from others is interrupted, you can get a collapse perhaps into depression. They struggle with deep questions about their self-worth, whether they're guilty of misdeeds, or bringing terrible things on themselves. They exaggerate their own responsibility.

Childhood Trauma in Adults

Despite deep, basic anxiety that people might have endured in childhood, they may come into their adult years and appear quite well on the surface apart from the evidence of their exaggerated defenses. Indeed, they can be extremely functional, intelligent, educated, hold down good jobs. But generally, they can't sustain long-term relationships very well. When they encounter a crisis, the other becomes the enemy too quickly and to an extreme degree. There's a rupture of the relationship as they cannot bear to be too close to potential enemies. Relationships become very difficult to maintain over a long period. Such people might not be so successful in types of jobs where you have to be a team player and work well with other people. As long as they can work by themselves, they may do well. Sometimes they're very creative and may find it best to work on their own and not bother too much with other people around them.

There are adults who endure fragile states that require ceaseless affirmation. If the flow of other people's acclaim is interrupted, even for brief periods, they can collapse into horrible depression. They may seek out ways to make themselves feel better through drugs or alcohol or other means of killing off the terrible feelings of low self-esteem, self-hate and self-accusation. If you're not being assured by a partner who's mirroring you, or the network of people who are in a work situation, I think the vulnerability to that kind of collapse is quite severe. They may lash out ferociously, and there is, of course, such a thing as narcissistic rage. If the mirroring isn't adequate or the mirroring from another person reveals a flaw or a fault, then the defenses can come into action that would appear in the form of an attack of rage designed to try to overcome the person (or enemy) who is pointing out their inadequacies. The problem is that when this person is confronted with an inadequacy, it confirms what they already know to be inadequacies. It's as if they're fighting against themselves, fighting against your own knowledge about yourself. It's a battle within and a battle without.

Substance Use Disorders (Addiction)

For some unfortunate people, substance use becomes a sort of balm for the troubled soul. However, the ego becomes enslaved in the throes of addiction. How do you understand that descent? When it becomes addiction, there is a metaphysical component to it, as if the body is craving for the substance and more. The ego is more or less helpless. The intensity of the addiction is greater than the amount of energy the ego has at its disposal to exert its will. Even people who want sobriety and want to stop using drugs often simply can't do it, that's why we have treatment centers to help them. It might be a terrible struggle to get rid of the physical addiction until the ego is able to make a free decision, but the descent into the addiction means the substance is working, that is, it is killing the pain, whether it's psychic pain or physical pain.

But it has another effect beyond helping the ego cope with pain because it introduces chemical dependency. Of course, there are also psychological addictions, where it's more of the ego question, and a strong ego can face the psychological part of the addiction. However, a weak ego is deeply helpless in the face of psychological addictions. It's usually a combination of a psychological and a physical addiction that puts people into clinics and treatment centers.

Higher Power and the Archetype

The first step of the 12-step program of Alcoholics Anonymous, a program that some people have associated with an encounter with Jung, involves admitting powerlessness. Oddly, the ego that is incapable of overcoming addiction is freed by acknowledging powerlessness. Just the first step of 12 steps, but it doesn't come from Jung.

There was a patient, Bill W., who came to see Jung after having relapsed into alcoholism. Jung realized that he couldn't cure this man. Psychotherapy, the kind he had to offer, was not going to do the job. So he said to him, "I can't help you. You have to look for a higher source of help." This man eventually began to meet with another person, and they developed the 12 steps, some of which were based on principles espoused by a Christian group, the Oxford Group. The first step was to say, "I'm helpless," and that was an echo of what Jung said: "I'm helpless. I can't help you." When Bill W. heard that, he turned to his inward self, saying, "I'm helpless. I can't help myself. I have to look for a higher power to help me," and that was the beginning of his developing the 12 steps and finding that higher power.

At the risk of stretching the apocryphal story too far, one may wonder if the ego, in its efforts to awaken, might not struggle with the same sort of drama. And in this case, the higher power could be akin to the Self.

I think what Jung was suggesting was that he as another human being couldn't help Bill W. Rather, Bill W. had to find a source within himself. And Bill

W. turned to the spiritual traditions that were available to him, biblical traditions. Prayer is part of it. You don't have to pray to a specific god image, but you have to look for a source beyond the ego itself. The ego's power is limited. Most of us think we have much more power than we actually have, but all you have to do is get sick or addicted or have something catastrophic happen to realize the limitations of the power that the ego has over its own house. What we realize is that instincts are powerful as well as the complexes and the Archetypes. These are mighty powers that can overtake us, possess us, and we're relatively helpless in their grips.

Keep in mind that sometimes it's OK to be possessed by the Archetypal powers. It gives us a sense of mission. It takes us somewhere that we need to go, gives a sense of location, perhaps, and a direction. Later, we become conscious of the power that we've been given through loan by the Archetypal sources of the psyche.

The ego itself is more like a mirror. It's a spark of consciousness. Jung sometimes compared it to a light in the darkness. You have a lantern, you're in a forest. It's nighttime, and you can only see so much around you. The forest is vast, and there are animals in the forest and ghosts and goblins and who knows what out there. And you've got your little light. That's the ego in the psyche.

Jung and Freud

Freud had a three-part structure to the psyche. The ego, the conscious will, which is similar to Jung. The id, that was for Freud the main domain of the instinctive unconscious. Finally, there's the superego, and that is the internalized sense of threat from father or the authorities that if we do something wrong, we will be punished. The superego kind of keeps us on track, culturally speaking. It's part of an anxiety system that's built into the psyche to be afraid of being punished, either by oneself with the feeling of guilt or by outer authorities if we're caught.

That was Freud's setup, and then the ego has to maintain or manage this conflict between what the id wants, (the instinctual desires) and what the superego wants (obedience to the rules, the morality of the culture and proper behavior).

Jung didn't set it up like that. Jung simply said the ego is the center of consciousness. It's subject to psychic forces and outside forces, including cultural forces that must be taken into account. Is there conflict? Yes, but it's more like a spot of consciousness or like a magnet that holds the contents of consciousness together.

Now, when we say "I," what is that? Jung says in one place in his late work the ego is a more or less stable configuration of several Archetypal components. Jung also says that the ego is the center of consciousness and that it is the mirror of the Self that is the center of the total psyche, and that the ego and the Self have an inherent mirroring connection. Erich Neumann spoke of the ego-Self axis. The connection between the ego and the Self, if it's stable, gives one a sense of inner security, reliability and stability. But the ego is very dependent on other people and other parts of the psyche supporting it, including the Self and other Archetypal energies.

Dream-ego and Waking-ego

In most dreams the "I," or what we call the dream-ego, is very similar to your sense of self when you're awake. When you recount the dream, you say, "I was walking down the road and I saw a lion coming out of the woods and I ran for cover." The "I" in the dream is very similar to the way you experience life in the waking state. So dream-ego and the waking-ego are not different in that case. But in some dreams, they're quite different.

I've seen some dreams of clients who dream that they are animals. One woman dreamed that she was a lion in St. Mark's Plaza in Venice, walking through the plaza. Another woman, I remember, dreamed that she was a butterfly. Sometimes you dream that you're another person or a different gender. Those are infrequent, but they do happen.

What we say about the dream is that it compensates for the waking state. Compensation means that it gives you something that you've left out or is lacking or you need in your ego consciousness in order to live closer to your full potential, your wholeness, or an improved state of consciousness. The dreams compensate by balancing that one-sidedness of consciousness.

If the dream-ego is very different, you would want to look at that difference. What is the dream-ego doing that waking conscious or the waking-ego, is not doing or cannot do? So in the case of the lion, it's giving a feeling of royalty and power to this person. You can say that in a waking state, the person maybe felt a lack of that kind of power. This is the power of the self; the lion is self-representation.

Now with the butterfly, that woman was too concrete, and the butterfly is anything but concrete. It's evanescent, it's ephemeral, it's the soul itself. She needed more lightness, a sense of self that had more symbolic value in her life. So, we looked at the difference and tried to interpret the ways in which the dream-ego was a compensation.

There was a German Jungian psychoanalyst, Hans Dieckmann, who wrote an essay on dream-ego in which he claimed that the dream-ego is more individuated than the waking-ego. That means that the dreaming ego can do things that the waking-ego couldn't do, or the dream-ego knows things that the waking-ego doesn't know and yet needs to know. He suggested the dream-ego is more advanced in consciousness and abilities than the waking-ego. I always try to keep that in the back of my mind when I think about this question: Is the dream-ego ahead of the waking-ego? Is it more developed; is it more individuated? It may even presage, sometimes, what the waking-ego is inclining toward.

Powerful Forces and Ego

The ego is afloat, adrift on an ocean of other forces that support and surround it. And sometimes, the winds are blowing in its favor, and sometimes, winds are blowing against it. If you read the great epics like *The Odyssey* or *The Aeneid*, you get this image of these sailors in boats, and if the gods are with them, everything is going fine, and then some god comes along and lets his anger out. Suddenly, there are high waves and hurricane-force winds, and a person is blown off course.

But that's a good picture of the ego, actually. It's in the midst of powerful forces that it can't control, but its strength is that it is awake. A resilient ego can survive a whole lot of difficulty and catastrophe going on around it. You see that in the heroes. Aeneas, in *The Aeneid* is one, as well as

Odysseus in *The Odyssey*. These are wonderful stories, showing how the ego copes with difficult environments as well as the gods and all the forces for and against it. These great stories serve to give us comfort during our own storms.

Collective Ego and BTS

There is a collective level at which ego comes into play. Every tightly knit group has a kind of collective ego that the individuals participate in. It doesn't mean the individuals don't have their own egos, especially when they're not in the group. They have their own separate individual egos, but they can also be very influenced by the group unconscious and the group orientation.

So, for instance, we have mob psychology, in which something about the individuals is taken up into an emotional state where their individual egos become melted together, so to speak, into a mob. Members of the mob participate in some extreme active thing that, left to their own devices, they would not engage in. Warfare is a bit like that, too. The army tries to instill its collective ego intention, led by the general to direct the troops what to do and how to behave. And the troops will follow that and carry out their orders and do things that, under normal circumstances, they would never consider, such as killing innocent people or people who are identified as enemies.

For example, BTS, the enormously popular group of seven singers, has become a sort of collective ego. Now BTS is not the kind of a group that engages in terrible things, but the members are very tightly knit. They practice together, they live together, they perform together, they travel together. So, I think there's a very closely and very carefully developed sense of that group identity that they all participate in. When one thinks, it's as though they all think. The songs are sung by one or another, but they represent the whole group.

That group identity influences them in their individual identities so even when they're apart, they still feel that they're part of the group. "I'm a BTS member," and that probably will never leave them because it's such an intense experience over a period of 10 years. During these formative years of adolescence and early adulthood, they form these intense bonds and a common purpose that will stay with them for the rest of their lives. Even when they go their separate ways. At some point, I'm sure they will. The group will break up, and the members will have their own separate, individual lives in a much fuller way than they have had until now.

Unus Mundus

The ego that is capable of becoming immersed during war or in the midst of a mob is also capable of being swept into mysteries like those that were practiced in antiquity. People seek out the experience of merger or ecstasy. This desire to merge into something larger, grander is fundamental. When you're really by yourself and alone, it can certainly be a very nice experience. Some people love to be alone. But in those moments, you also realize how small you are in relation to the bigger scheme of things. And when you merge with another, you lose that sense of separateness. You enter into an experience of oneness with all that is.

Freud wrote about this. He said that when people fall in love, the ego loses its boundaries, and they become one. It's an experience of oneness and unity that is marvelous. Most people, when they are in love, feel at one with the world and everything that is. It's like that experience of union.

We speak about the *unus mundus* and the *anima mundi*. The experience of union with another individual or group gives you the experience of unity with the world. Some may think of that as a repeat of an experience of the reality you had when you were in your mother's womb. In the womb, there were no divisions or separation. All was one. Others may think of it as a very advanced stage of knowing that at a certain level, everything is one. It's all energy, we're all united, we're all a part of everything; this is a kind of advanced mystical state.

Ultimately, we all long for that and search for it. We find it and experience it in love, or in religious experiences, or sometimes in a dream that is like a vision of unity of all that is. Love is the glue that holds things together. Hate is the force that separates. So they're at war with each other, love and hate. They're both necessary, but that experience of oneness is something everybody longs for.

Chapter 12

Music: The Universal Language

By Leonard Cruz

"Music is the universal language of mankind."
Henry Wadsworth Longfellow

The rich artistry of BTS's latest album speaks for itself precisely because Longfellow was right that music is the universal language. The proof is the enormous worldwide appeal that BTS has across so many cultures and languages. Their latest album reverberates with deep psychological strains. It is a most unusual phenomenon that Dr. Murray Stein's writings has been a source of inspiration for BTS and in turn their albums have inspired Dr. Stein to reflect so deeply on the meaning of their lyrics and artistry. We wait to see if the album *Map of the Soul: 7* will prove to be the culmination of this series of circular causal feedbacks loops or dialogues between an author and analyst in the seasoned phase of his life and a group of seven young men whose insight and self-awareness is unexpectedly seasoned already.

Perhaps it would be more accurate to claim that music that deals with universal themes is the universal language of mankind. While BTS is fashioned in the tradition of Korean Pop, this misses the fact that even within a genre there are artists whose reach is broad, deep, and speaks to all of us. BTS has shown itself to be such artists. Whether or not BTS fans, the ARMY, ever study the rich, textured meaning of each album track that Dr. Stein illuminated in this book, they will be deeply touched by the themes. Therein lies another mystery about how music speaks to us. There are themes we first encounter in a song that we don't recognize as universal until life experience seasons us and reveals something we may have first encountered in a song. And of course, many of us can mark the epochs of our life with the music we listened to at certain points in time.

I am a fan of all sorts of Reggae music. But when I hear Bob Marley sing "Redemption Song" something in me is awakened; it is that indominable element of the human spirit that rises from oppression. These lyrics combined with his soulful voice communicate with my soul in the most profound ways.

> Old pirates, yes, they rob I
> Sold I to the merchant ships
> Minutes after they took I
> From the bottomless pit
>
> But my hand was made strong
> By the hand of the almighty
> We forward in this generation
> Triumphantly

My heritage does not include ancestors brought to the Americas in slave ships but I've known my own sort of oppression from which only the hand of an almighty has delivered me.

Perhaps the most intriguing feature of the back and forth between BTS and Dr. Stein is the possibility that a younger generation has been invited to encounter Carl Jung and maybe explore the inner life somewhat earlier than is common. A careful observer will recognize that a lack of psychological curiosity is a condition afflicting many people in positions of power. World leaders, celebrities, and spiritual and religious leaders sometimes show an astounding deficit of self-awareness. They are often quite self-interested but that is not the same as being interested in the self (or SELF).

Sadly, when politicians, celebrities and spiritual leaders have not undertaken the work of individuation, they are more likely to work out their psychological struggles at the expense of others. This is true of each of us, the only difference being that politicians, celebrities, and spiritual leaders have a larger sphere of influence over which they can spread harm or benefit. When a group whose popularity likely exceeds that of the Beetles shines a spotlight on the work of individuation, we all benefit. If even one of their fans embarks on a serious examination of the themes in their song that are expounded using only words in this book, then BTS will likely have made the world a better place. The impact that might result from thousands of BTS's fans taking stock of themselves and plumbing the depths of their inner lives can scarcely be overstated.

The hope for this book is that the marriage of the album and the book might deepen the experience of both for the listener and reader. Let me close with a part of a stanza and a part of the refrain from "Redemption Song".

Emancipate yourselves from mental
slavery
None but ourselves can free our mind
(…)
Won't you help to sing
These songs of freedom?
'Cause all I ever had
Redemption songs

Endnotes

[i] Interview with Laura London in answer to questions presented by BTS related to Jung's Map of the Soul, Open Court, Peru IL, 1998.

[ii] Stein, Murray, The Principles of Individuation, Chiron Publications, Asheville, NC, 2015, p 13-15.

[iii] Jacoby, Mario, The Analytic Encounter, Inner City, Toronto, Canada, 1984, p 118.

[iv] Otsuka, Y, Face Recognition in Infants: A review of behavioural and near-infrared spectroscopic studies, Japanese Psychological Research, 2014, Volume 56 No. 1, 76-90.

www.ingramcontent.com/pod-product-compliance
Lightning Source LLC
Chambersburg PA
CBHW021619270326
41931CB00008B/765